SPEED CLEANING

SPEED CLEANING

A spotless house in just 15 minutes a day

Shannon Lush & Jennifer Fleming

EBURY PRESS

1 3 5 7 9 10 8 6 4 2

First published in 2006 by ABC Books for the AUSTRALIAN BROADCASTING CORPORATION

This edition published in 2008 by Ebury Press, an imprint of Ebury Publishing

A Random House Group Company

The Random House Group Limited Reg. No. 954009

Addresses for companies within the Random House Group can be found at www.random-
house.co.uk

A CIP catalogue record for this book is available from the British Library

The Random House Group Limited supports The Forest Stewardship Council (FSC), the
leading international forest certification organisation. All our titles that are printed on
Greenpeace approved FSC certified paper carry the FSC logo. Our paper procurement policy
can be found at www.rbooks.co.uk/environment

To buy books by your favourite authors and register for offers visit www.rbooks.co.uk

Printed and bound by CPI Mackays, Chatham ME5 8TD

ISBN 9780091922573

Designed by saso content & design pty ltd
Illustrations by Ian Faulkner

CONTENTS

KEY TO SYMBOLS

You will find that different types of cleaning information are included in this book. To make finding the correct cleaning tips easier, we've included symbols and boxes.

 Broom symbol This is your speedcleaning guide

 Glove symbol This helps with setting up strategies to make cleaning easier and speedier.

 Flower symbol This is your Spring and Autumn Cleaning Guide

 Hints box General hints are boxed like this

'Priceless' box Hints from yesteryear are boxed like this.

If you think your cleaning is slow...

HOW TO ... FROM *LEE'S PRICELESS RECIPES*, 1817

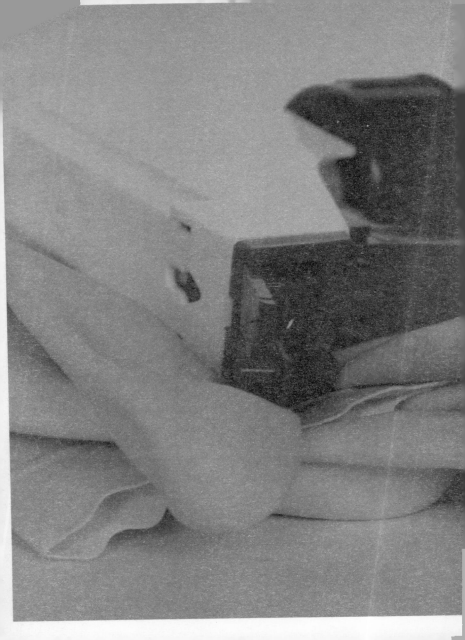

How to Speedclean

WHY SPEED CLEANING?

These days, everyone is flat out and on the go. The last thing you want to do at the end of a hectic day is clean the house. It's why we've devised Speedcleaning. It's for people who want a clean house but are time-poor. The approach can be summed up in one word – systems. Having systems in place will mean your house will run more smoothly and efficiently. The best news is that with some organisation and 15 minutes a day, you can transform your cleaning routine!

WHO ARE WE?

For those readers who are not familiar with the book *Spotless*, Shannon Lush is a fine art restorer who knows how to repair anything, whether it's an expensive antiquity or a favourite aunt's vase. Shannon is also a keen collector of handy household hints, a lifelong passion that has been handed down through generations. Not only does she collect hints, she also tests and modifies them to make them even better. Shannon is also known as the 'Queen of Clean', appearing as a regular guest on radio and television across Australia and New Zealand. She helps listeners with all manner of domestic disasters and has never been stumped.

Jennifer Fleming is a presenter and producer on ABC Radio and has worked with Australia's leading journalists and commentators. Jen first met Shannon over the telephone – when Shannon rang James Valentine's Afternoon Show on 702 ABC Sydney as a talkback caller. Week after week, people would ring for help with new spills and stains and Shannon would have an answer for every problem. Jen noticed there was a huge interest in non-toxic remedies and a desire to remember old-fashioned tips and advice. She approached Shannon with the idea of writing a book. Once *Spotless* was released, people started asking if there was another book. They wanted information on cleaning techniques, and that is how *Speed Cleaning* came to life. Like most listeners and readers, Jen doesn't know a lot about stains and cleaning, but she's good at asking the right questions and extracting the best information from Shannon's encyclopaedic database brain. It's a perfect collaboration.

We hope you'll keep *Speed Cleaning* next to *Spotless* on the bookshelf and use the two in tandem.

JENNIFER'S ACKNOWLEDGEMENTS

Many people have assisted in the creation of this book. Thanks to James Valentine from 702 ABC Sydney for allowing it to begin. Thanks to Susan Morris-Yates, Megan Johnston, Nanette Backhouse, Ian Faulkner, Stuart Neal, Jane Finemore and the team at ABC Books for their contribution. Family and friends have given so much support. Particular thanks to John and Pat Fleming, Tony Speede and Jodi McKay. Thanks also to Amanda Woods who relayed the advice about spiders and lemons in the first place. Thank you to Elizabeth Troyeur – and, of course, to the Queen of Clean, Shannon Lush.

SHANNON'S ACKNOWLEDGEMENTS

I'd like to add my thanks to all those that Jennifer listed, and to add a few more. To the women of my family, Eleanor Saich (my wonderful mum), Bronwyn Macinante and Narelle Dean (my supportive sisters), Tamara Custance and Erin Lush (my beautiful daughters) and my aunts and grandmother and all the rest. And to the men of my family, John Referendum Hayes (my dad), Trent Hayes, John Hayes Jr (my brothers) and so many more that I could fill a book just with the names of my loving, supportive and inspirational family.

My ABC family – James Valentine, Richard Fidler, Carole Whitelock, Bernadette Young, Louise Saunders, Annie Gastin, Alison Buchanan, Bonita Brown, Scott Levi, Madeleine Randall, Aaron Kearney, all the producers and technical staff, publicists, publishers, way too many to list.

A special thank you to all the listeners and readers. I've enjoyed meeting so many of you.

I can't bypass big thank yous to Jennifer Fleming – a friend and collaborator.

And last but definitely not least my wonderful husband Rick who not only puts up with a workaholic wife, but aids and abets her.

Setting Up the House

SETTING UP THE HOUSE

Can you find a spare 15 minutes a day? That's all the time it will take to speedclean a standard room in a house. Sounds too easy, doesn't it? Well, there may be some initial changes you'll have to make before you reach top speed, but once you do, you too could become a lean, mean, speedcleaning machine!

In this book we outline three types of cleaning: daily cleaning, speedcleaning and spring/autumn cleaning. Daily cleaning includes jobs like wiping worktops, washing dishes, sorting laundry and emptying bins. Speedcleaning includes weekly and emergency cleaning. Spring/autumn cleaning is done only twice a year and is like a stocktake or audit of the household. We'll take you through the house, room by room, outlining speedcleaning techniques as well as describing how to make general cleaning speedier. We also anticipate cleaning emergencies and include lots of tips and hints for around the home.

Here are the basic rules for speedcleaning:

10 STEPS FOR EACH ROOM

Follow this order to speedclean each room.

1. Assemble the clean kit.
2. Declutter the room and empty wastepaper bin.
3. Dust ceiling and light fittings.
4. Dust walls and tops of cupboards/bookshelves/wardrobes.
5. Dust paintings, hangings and other wall features.
6. Clean light switches, door jambs and window sills.
7. Clean furniture.
8. Clean floors.
9. Do refills, arrange fresh flowers, add fragrance and what I call froufrou, or frilly things, such as doilies.
10. Empty the clutter bucket. Put away your clean kit. Adjust the master list (the list of long-term cleaning needs).

A PLACE FOR EVERYTHING, AND EVERYTHING IN ITS PLACE

No matter what the item is, everything – from sticky tape to DVDs – needs to have a designated spot. Putting things in their special place will not only speed up your cleaning, but life inside the house will be easier because you won't be searching high and low for whatever you need. The best way to work out where to keep things is to start with some graph paper, a tape measure, a pencil, scissors and plain paper. Graph paper is becoming increasingly hard to find so another option is to print off a sample from the back of this book (see page 208). Pick a room in your house and measure the furniture. Represent the room to scale on graph paper and work out the corresponding size of your furniture to scale. You'll find a sample at the rear of this book. Create flat cutout models of your furniture using scissors and plain paper. You can arrange and rearrange the furniture in the room until you work out the best layout. Keep your paper cutouts in a zip-lock bag in case you want to rearrange the room again or if you move house. If paper cutouts aren't your thing, you could also use a pencil and draw the furniture directly onto the graph paper, but it's harder to move around if you change your mind.

When working out your floor plan, take into account the breezeways in each room. They will be different for each house and each room. To determine a breezeway, light a candle and see in which direction the flame blows. The flame will bend away from the breeze indicating how the air circulates. What you're

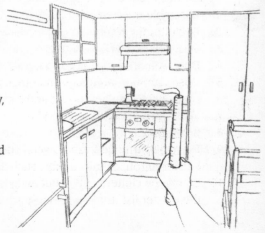

aiming for is air to flow as easily as possible: so don't put a heavy item of furniture near a window if it blocks the flow of air. Good airflow helps to prevent mould and creates a much healthier atmosphere – and it's cooler in summer.

While arranging a room, think about creating the smallest walking distance between two points; which means items should be stored near where they are used. For example, scissors could be kept in a kitchen drawer or in an office drawer, or you may decide to have two pairs if they are used often in both locations. You don't want to be going backwards and forwards constantly. Another example is cutlery, which should be stored near the dishwasher or dish rack so you don't have to move far to put it away. For items that don't have a regular home, set up a miscellaneous bowl or basket. Just make sure you clear it out regularly.

If there are several people in your home, consider colour coding. The way this works is that everyone in the house is allocated their own colour and that colour is then attached to their items. For shared items, there's a household colour. By using this method, the household has a system for sorting and storing things.

A small bit of advice: no matter how enthusiastic you are, don't overwhelm yourself and attempt to overhaul the whole house in one go. Take it one room at a time!

'Hints for Blokes' are included throughout the book because men and women clean differently. Men generally clean from one side of a room to another whereas women tend to be more job-specific. Men tend to be visual when cleaning, so make sure their line-of-sight is unimpaired. They may need to stand on a ladder or sit on the floor to see the dirt. Women tend to clean because they know it's there, even if they can't see it – they'll rewash clothes because they're in the dirty pile rather than because they need it. There are pluses and minuses in both ways of cleaning. Neither style is better – they're just different. Allow for these differences in approach.

DO A LITTLE BIT OFTEN

It's easy to let things pile up, but really, you're just creating more work for yourself. Keep in mind that old saying: 'a stitch in time saves nine'. It's better to have one pile than nine! And let's be honest: no matter how busy you are, you can always find some time in your day if you really want to. Schedule it in if you need to.

The speedcleaning routine is based around a nine-room house. The idea is to clean one room per weekday and four rooms on Saturday with a day off on Sunday, or whenever you'd like it to be. You may prefer to clean the whole house one day each week. It's up to you to work out the system that suits you best. Add 10–15 minutes extra time for each additional person in the house per day because more people mean more mess. The important thing is to have a system and for that system to be as efficient as possible.

I also think it's crucial that everyone in the house knows the system so it's not a 'one-person rule' situation – because that one person then tends to get a bit cranky. Assign the worst or laziest cleaner in the house to coordinate the schedule because they'll be more likely to follow their own rules. Also, you can't get cross with a list!

HAVE THE RIGHT CLEANING TOOLS FOR THE JOB

I can't emphasise enough just how important it is to have the right cleaning tools for the job. Storing the tools in the nearest location will keep cleaning time to a minimum. There are several ways to organise your clean kit. You could have everything stored at a centralised spot or divided up and kept in different parts of the house. You could have different kits for different rooms. You might like to carry items in buckets or plastic toolboxes or you may even use a trolley like they do in hotels. It depends on your storage situation and preferences. I like to be able to pick up my clean kit with one hand – and have found that a nappy bucket is the perfect size for me. I

attach a butcher's hook (available from hardware shops) to the edge of the bucket so I can hang a rag from it. Whatever you decide to use, just make sure the kit isn't too heavy.

Another suggestion is to store a cloth for cleaning wood in a zip-lock bag in the family room, for example. That way, when you've got a spare couple of minutes or when you're talking on the phone, you could speedclean some furniture. The main thing is to have your kit ready to go for the speedclean.

If you don't have a broom cupboard, create a storage area by fixing hooks from the hardware shop on the back of doors or in cupboards.

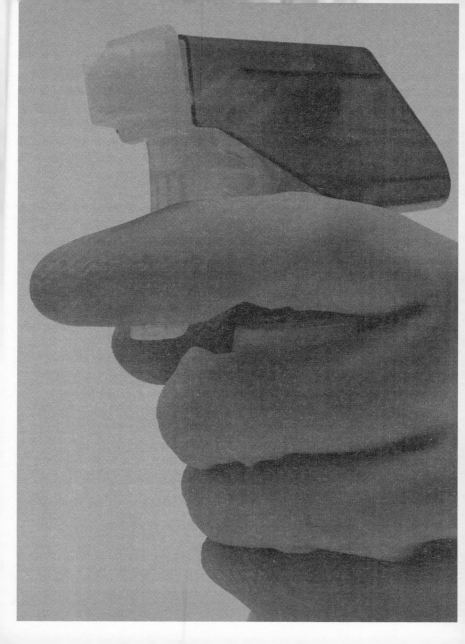

Brooms come in many varieties, including nylon, straw, copra, bristle and polycarbonate. Select the broom according to the surface and amount of soil to remove. As a general rule, the heavier the soiling, the tougher the broom required. They can be long-handled or short-handled. Nylon brooms have soft bristles and are best used inside the house. If you wrap an old T-shirt around the head of a long-handled nylon broom, it can also be used as a mop. Straw brooms are good for outside the house to sweep bulky dust and to collect cobwebs. Yard brooms have a wider head and are good for large areas such as driveways, paths, verandahs, garage floors and patios. If you can, clean the broom every time you use it. Do this by wetting a bar of soap with water then rub it over the broom bristles. Rinse the broom under warm water, shake the excess water off then stand the broom upwards to dry. Brooms are quite cheap these days so have several. You could even colour code them!

Buckets come in many shapes and colours. Square, oblong and round are the most common shapes. Round buckets are either standard or nappy size. Choose ones with a pouring spout and lid. Use buckets to soak clothes, store washing water and transport items.

Clothes' baskets aid the transport of clothes. They can be plastic, cane or wicker. Never have one bigger than you can lift when full. Plastic ones are light, come in a variety of colours and are easily cleaned with a little washing-up liquid on a damp cloth. Cane baskets are popular but wear more quickly, take less weight and, because they're unsealed, collect mould. Wicker baskets are rarely made any more but Shannon loves them. Wash them with salt water applied with a cloth every two months. When not in use, store all baskets upside down, so they don't collect dust.

Cloths come in many varieties, but the best cloth is an old cotton T-shirt or old cotton knickers with the gusset cut out. Both are lint-free and can be washed in a washing machine on a hot setting. You can use proprietary cloths but there's no need to. See the Rag Bag (page 12) for other types of cloths.

Clutter bucket is any kind of handled bucket used to transport items from one room to another. Select whichever size suits you best. I find allocating a particular colour for each family member is a good organisational approach.

Dusters I think the best duster is an old cotton T-shirt because it picks up dirt really well, is easy to wash out and won't scratch surfaces. Fluffy dusters tend to spread the dirt around the house so it just settles elsewhere. The best way to dust is to wipe a damp cloth over a surface. When we say damp, this means the cloth has been wrung out so tightly that it feels cool against your skin. If it's wet, you can feel the moisture and the water will end up creating mud trails when you clean. When storing a dusting cloth, wring it out in methylated spirits to make it antiseptic and sterile. Once it's dry, put it away with your clean kit ready to use next time. Never wipe surfaces directly with methylated spirits!

Dustpan and brush collect dust, dirt, leaves and other items.

Elastic bands are used to temporarily secure items. They need to be strong enough for the job. Here they are mainly used to secure T-shirts over a broom head or vacuum cleaner.

Gloves can be disposable, rubber, cotton, gardening, polyurethane or acid-resistant. They protect the skin from chemicals, abrasion and heat and can also help with grip.

Hairdryer is very useful for dusting, particularly delicate fine china. A hairdryer also helps to remove wax and can be used to apply heat to an area to speed up the drying process.

Mop can be made of rag or sponge, although newer ones combine the two and have spongy rags. I prefer to put an old T-shirt over a broom head and use that as a mop because it's easier to clean and clean with.

Old stockings are great cleaners and good non-scratch scourers, especially when cutting through soap scum. They're also handy to wrap around the back of taps to clean. And they're cheap to buy if you don't have any old ones around the house.

Old toothbrushes – don't throw them away! Keep them to clean difficult-to-access areas, such as around taps and in tight corners.

Old T-shirts are great to use for mopping, dusting, polishing and wrapping over the vacuum cleaner head to protect surfaces. They're also very absorbent. If you don't have any old T-shirts, buy them cheaply at second-hand shops, which is cheaper than buying new sponges at the supermarket.

Paper towels are great for mopping up spills and clearing grease.

Rag bags can be used for storing old T-shirts, clothes, tea towels and towels to use as rags for cleaning. Old woollen jumpers are great furniture polishers. Just make sure you remove all buttons and recycle them in your button box. Make your own rag bag using an old pillowcase and simply attach it with hooks, tacks or screws to the inside of a cupboard or the back of a door.

Rubbish bags come in a variety of sizes, strengths and thicknesses. Whether you have tie tops or drawstring bags is your choice.

Scrubbing brush has a wooden or plastic top, and tough bristles. A washing-up brush, made of nylon or bristles, can be used as a scrubbing brush. Use on stubborn stains and in tight corners.

Sponges – use different coloured sponges so you don't contaminate your areas. I use green sponges on worktops, pink sponges on the floor and yellow and blue sponges in the bathroom. Wash sponges in a small bowl of white vinegar, leave overnight then rinse in hot water.

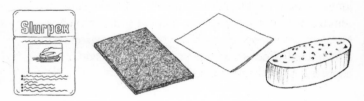

Spray bottles can be bought at the supermarket or reuse an old spray bottle – buy the cheapest product that comes in a refillable spray bottle, use the product, clean the bottle in warm water then reuse. Check the bottle has a spray or mist option on the nozzle. Use removable labels and mark the bottle clearly. Spray bottles have many uses, for example, fill with lavender oil and water to use as an air-freshener in the toilet.

Squeegee is a short-handled rubber-bladed implement used to wipe water from a surface. It operates like a windscreen wiper on a car. Use it to clean windows, the shower screen in the bathroom or to pick up dropped eggs from the kitchen floor. A squeegee can be bought at the supermarket, hardware or discount shop.

Storage box could be an old cardboard box, plastic box or wooden crate in a variety of shapes and sizes. Select one according to its use.

Vacuum cleaner – what a great invention! It sucks up dust and dirt from all manner of things using a variety of attachments. The main elements of the vacuum cleaner are:

+barrel: this is the body of the cleaner. It has an inlet and outlet connection. The inlet is where the hose goes and it sucks dirt into the barrel. The outlet is where the air blows out of the machine and it's generally covered. You can attach the hose to the outlet to backflush and clean the vacuum cleaner.

+bag: located inside the barrel. Modern vacuum cleaners have a window which shows when the bag is full. If you don't have this, check the bag each time you use the cleaner. It's a good idea to change the bag regularly. The vacuum cleaner won't work efficiently if the bag is more than half full.

+tube: hard part – the length may be varied to suit your height or according to what you're vacuuming. Make it shorter when vacuuming furnishings and longer when vacuuming floors. If you are tall, extra lengths are available from the vacuum cleaner shop and will save your back.

+soft part – the flexible hose connection.

+main head: this can be set to have bristles up or down. Vacuum with the bristles down for shiny and hard floors; put the bristles up for carpets and soft floors, unless you have pets. Clean any fur or dust out of the bristles with an old comb.

+brush head: a small round attachment with long bristles designed to clean cobwebs, cornices, window sills, etc.

+upholstery nozzle: a small flat attachment to be used to vacuum the surface of furnishings, curtains and pelmets.

+corner nozzle: use it to access tight spaces, such as the sides of chairs, or to clean around the buttons on padded furniture.

VACUUMING TECHNIQUE

Work from the top of the room to the bottom. Begin vacuuming with the brush head and remove cobwebs from the ceiling. Then clean the tops of things such as wardrobes, picture rails, dado rails, skirting boards, light fittings, window frames and sills and so on. Then change to the corner nozzle and vacuum skirting boards, corners and edges. Attach the main head and clean under furniture before vacuuming the main areas. Start in one corner of the room and move diagonally across – vacuuming diagonally puts less stress on the carpet fibres and leaves fewer marks. Just before you finish vacuuming, spray some insecticide spray onto a tissue then suck it up into the cleaner to kill any insects that might have landed in the bag. Alternatively, you could put some oil of pennyroyal on a tissue and suck it into the bag. (**Do not use pennyroyal if anyone in the house is pregnant.**) If you're allergic to dust mites, suck a couple of damp teabags into the vacuum cleaner bag before you start cleaning. This will kill the dust mites.

HINT

To clean the vacuum cleaner, vacuum inside the barrel and all the attachments and clean the outside with a damp cloth. Wash the head in a mild washing-up liquid solution but make sure you dry it well so that it doesn't rust or corrode.

CLEANING SCHEDULE/LISTS

Even if there's only one person in your house, a cleaning schedule is really helpful because you'll always know where you are in the cleaning routine. I always start cleaning at the front of the house where the main bedroom is and work in one direction around the house: that way I don't track dirt and I can remember where I'm up to.

As an example, here's my cleaning planner.

Monday – bedrooms
Tuesday – lounge/dining
Wednesday – bathrooms
Thursday – kitchen
Friday – family/study
Saturday – entrance/hall/outside/laundry
Sunday – day off

Make a master cleaning list that includes dates for when you shampooed the carpet, had equipment serviced, cleaned windows, fixed squeaky locks and hinges, had pest inspections, checked exterior paintwork and completed minor repairs so that you know when you next need to address that issue. If you've just had your carpets steam cleaned, don't spot clean for at least four weeks and then vacuum the area four times because the chemicals used in steam cleaning can adversely interact with them. When you're speedcleaning, you'll come across tasks, such as stains and scratches that you won't be able to deal with at the time. Write these down and add them to the master list. When you have some spare time, you can consult the list and do the task. If you have children, include them on the roster and reward small children with a stamp or a gold star and older children with a treat for a job well done. Helping with regular chores is a good way for kids to earn pocket money.

There are several ways to store the cleaning list. Attach it to the fridge with a magnet or keep a book with the information stored near your cleaning kit. For speedcleaning, I use two A4-sized magnetic sheets, which you can buy from hardware and craft shops. One magnetic sheet has the master Lush Family Cleaning Roster on it, which I mark with a whiteboard marker. The other magnetic sheet has been cut into shapes with various irregular jobs written and drawn on them, for example, there's a magnet for shampooing the carpet. This magnet is placed on top of the master roster until the job is done. Be as creative as you like – cut pictures from magazines or photographs of family members and glue them to the magnetic shapes. These shapes can be used to stick on the master sheet to show what job has been completed and by whom. Kids love them and will enjoy helping to make them.

REWARDS

If you find cleaning a real chore, set up some incentives and rewards to help you. Play your favourite music (I always knew an old neighbour of mine was cleaning when loud disco music was playing!). Sing at the top of your voice. Listen to a podcast. If you're the competitive type, make cleaning an Olympic event by setting an alarm and trying to beat your personal best. Imagine your mother is about to visit. You could even pretend you're an actor in a play about cleaning. Once you've completed the cleaning, allow yourself some treats for work well done. Buy yourself a bunch of flowers or pick some from the garden, play a computer game, sit down and watch the footy, have a cuppa or do whatever makes you feel relaxed. If you've got cleaning tasks you just detest, tackle them first before moving on to the ones you detest less. Make difficult jobs a challenge, not a chore. I have a friend who does one difficult job a day to keep these tasks under control. There's an added bonus to doing this: you'll feel great when you've completed the task and the other members in the house will feed off your positive energy.

KNOW YOUR SURFACES

When choosing a cleaning product, you have to know what the stain is and what surface you're working with. For instance, is your wooden table bare timber or does it have a polyurethane, shellac, varnish or acrylic finish? If you don't know, you need to find out. The same goes for any surface you're working with: be it fabric, vinyl, leather or even carpet. They all react in different ways to different products and cleaning utensils. To work out what the surface has been sealed with, take a pin or needle, hold it in a pair of pliers and heat it on the stove. Touch the pin to an inconspicuous part of the table and smell the fume it creates. If it smells like burning plastic, it's polyurethane. If it smells like an electrical firt, it's an oil-based varnish. If it smells like burning hair it's shellac. If it smells like a snuffed candle, it's waxed. To repair polyurethane, apply a little Brasso with a cloth and and rub in the direction of the grain over the mark. You should rub fast not hard. It will look worse before it looks better! Shellac, varnish and wax can be repaired using warm beeswax applied with the yellow side of a piece of lemon peel.

WHAT THINGS ARE

Acetone is a volatile, flammable ketone. It's used as a solvent for resins, primers, nail polish and heavy plastics. It can also be used to strip polyurethane, but be careful because it's very strong. It's available from the chemist or hardware shop.

Beeswax is the wax produced by bees when making honeycomb. It's a great polishing agent for sealed (except polyurethane) or unsealed wood finishes.

Bicarb is bicarbonate of soda, sodium bicarbonate or bi-carb soda. It's a salt and an alkaline that neutralises acid. It penetrates stains and dissolves grease on many different surfaces. It's available at the super-market, generally in the cake-baking rather than the cleaning aisle, and the chemist.

Bleach is a whitening agent that weakens fibres. It makes stiff linen become fine linen.

Blu-tak is a putty-like proprietary product used to temporarily adhere one surface to another. It can also be used to clean dirt from hard-to-reach areas.

Borax is a crystalline sodium borate that can be used as a fungicide, insecticide and detergent booster. It is mildly toxic: avoid contact with skin and do not ingest it. It is available from the chemist.

Bran is the ground husk of wheat or other grains. It's absorbent and can be used as a scourer. It is good for cleaning fabric, fur, silver or silver-plated items.

Brasso is a proprietary product. It's an abrasive and a metal polish and can be used to partially melt and polish polyurethane and polyethylene surfaces.

Camphor is a ketone from the camphor laurel tree. It has a strong vapour that moths and cats don't like. It's very flammable so never heat it.

Carpet cleaners come in many varieties. They can be soap-based, bicarb-based, detergent-based or alcohol-based. Be careful cleaning your carpets after they've been steam cleaned because there can be adverse chemical reactions.

Chamois block fine-grade cleaning block that is a very absorbent sponge. It removes moisture from carpet and other surfaces. Punch make one.

Cloves are a spice that come from the dried flower buds of the clove tree. Cloves deter silverfish and moths and are great for cupboards and bookshelves.

Cornflour is a starch from maize, rice and other grains. It's absorbent and a very fine abrasive.

Denture soaker can be used to clean and remove stubborn grey marks on porcelain. It can also clean craze marks on china and remove fruit and plant stains from terracotta.

Descaler removes limescale and calcium deposits from kettles, coffee machines, steam irons, shower heads, toilets and sinks. It's available in various forms from the supermarket or hardware shops.

Detergent is the liquid used when washing kitchen paraphernalia by hand. It emulsifies grease and oils making them easier to remove.

Dry cleaning fluid is also known as white spirits. It's a solvent and is available from hardware shops.

Epsom salts are hydrated magnesium sulphate and are so named because they were found at Epsom in Surrey. They are good for soaking aching limbs in the bath, for unshrinking woollens and for magnesium-deficient plants.

Eucalyptus oil is an essential oil distilled from the leaves of certain eucalyptus trees. It's a paint stripper, adhesive solvent and releases vapours. It's available from the supermarket or chemist.

Fuller's Earth is high-calcium clay with a bleaching action. It's very absorbent and acts as a wool relaxant, so it can be used to shrink or unshrink woollens or remove sweat from felt or to block hats. It's available at the chemist.

Goanna oil is rendered goanna fat used to restore glass that has glass cancer. It's very difficult to find but may be available at the chemist.

Glycerine is an odourless, clear liquid. It's used as an agent in cosmetics, toothpaste and shampoos and helps to loosen stains. It's available at the supermarket or chemist.

Graphite puffer is used to unstick locks and hinges. Graphite is a dry lubricant similar to a finely shaved lead pencil minus the clay. The puffer bulb allows access to tight areas.

Gumption is a whitish-grey cleaning paste which has many uses. It's great for cleaning baths and sinks. It contains a mild bleaching agent and abrasive. It's available at the supermarket.

Hydrogen peroxide is an oxidising liquid used as an antiseptic and bleaching agent. It's available at the supermarket or chemist.

Lavender oil is derived from lavender flowers and has many uses, including insect repellent, dog inhibitor, air freshener and toilet cleaner. It's available at the supermarket or chemist.

Leather dew is a combination of soap and oil that is used to treat leather. It is available from the shoe repair shop.

Lemon oil comes from the oil in lemon peel and is used as a furniture polish, spider and insect inhibitor and stain remover, as well as for its fragrance and flavour.

Methylated spirits is a raw alcohol with menthol. It's a solvent for some paints and can also be used to disinfect surfaces. The alcohol kills most bacteria but should never be applied to a wooden surface. It's available at the supermarket or hardware store.

Oil of cloves is cold-pressed oil from the dried flower buds of the

clove tree. It's a mould inhibitor, insecticide –
particularly for silverfish – toothache soother and
cooking ingredient. It's available from the chemist.

Oil of pennyroyal is oil from a small-leafed mint. It deters moths,
fleas and hard-shell insects, such as beetles and
millipedes, **but is harmful to pregnant women and
animals and shouldn't be used by them or near
them.** Pennyroyal can be difficult to obtain but you
can always get living plants from your nursery.

Plaster of Paris is a white powder made of calcium sulphate. It
forms a paste when mixed with water and can be
shaped before setting. It's also absorbent and is
good for removing stains from granite and pavers
when applied in thin layers. It's available from art
supply shops and hardware shops.

Salt is an abrasive, a disinfectant and kills mould.
When cleaning, use non-iodised table salt, coarse
cooking salt or swimming pool salt, which are
cheaper.

Scotchgard is a fabric protector. It creates a water-impermeable
coating to prevent spills and stains from
penetrating fabrics without affecting the look or feel
of the fabric.

Shellac is a varnish made from the resin of the Coccus
Lacca scale insect. The resin is dissolved in alcohol
or a similar solvent and used for making varnish,
polish and sealing wax.

Soap (bar of soap) used for general cleaning. The only
difference between the cheap and expensive ones is
the perfumes, oils and moisturisers used in them.
Cheap ones are fine for cleaning and often better.

Soap flakes are very thin pure flakes of soap. You can buy

them as flakes or grate a bar of soap. You
could also use a soap shaker for the same result.
A soap shaker is a wire box with a handle.
Place a bar of soap inside, clip it shut and run water
through it or shake it in water to generate suds.

Soap powder is washing powder used for washing clothes in the
washing machine.

Surex Oxysure is a pool cleaning chemical and an alternative to
chlorine. It kills algae, including mildew, and is
great for cleaning paths.

Sweet almond oil is the oil extracted from almond nuts. It's used to
clean bone and ivory and lubricate glass. It can be
used to remove glass stoppers in decanters. It's
available at supermarkets and chemists.

Talcum powder is an absorbent, a lubricant and a fine-grade
abrasive. It can be used for polishing, absorbing
stains or soothing babies' bottoms. It also helps
prevent rubber from perishing. I use talcum powder
to determine the tracks of ants and fleas.

Tea unless specified, use black, Indian tea. Tea contains
tannins, which are good for cleaning aluminium,
killing dust mites and inhibiting insects. It's also a
great pick-me-up when sipped!

Tea tree oil is an oil extracted from tea tree bushes. It's used as
an antibacterial and solvent for oil-based paints. It
removes resin stains, such as sticky tape residue
and wax.

Unibond PVA is a PVA wood glue and sealant.

Vanilla essence is the product of extract from vanilla beans
combined with alcohol. It is used to provide
fragrance and flavour to food and as a deodoriser.
If you run out of perfume, dab behind your ears and

you might get your neck nibbled. It is available from the supermarket.

Vanish   is a soaking agent that comes in several varieties. Vanish Oxi Action Crystal White removes some proteins, oils, organic or petrochemical stains, but can only be used if the item being cleaned is white. Vanish Oxi Action can be used on colours as well as whites and is good for tannin stains, protein, fats and oil stains. Vanish Pre Wash is great for mystery stains and for underarm deodorant stains. Use Vanish as a soaker, powder or create a paste by adding water.

Vaseline   is petroleum jelly that is used as a lubricant, a water barrier and to stop snails getting into your window boxes.

Vinegar   is an acid. It's a preservative, condiment, beverage, cleaner and sanitiser. Cider vinegar is best on hard surfaces that are not colour sensitive. Don't use it on white tiles, white laminex or anything that is lighter than the colour of the cider vinegar. White vinegar is better for cleaning light-coloured surfaces, such as white marble and fabric. Both are available from the supermarket.

White spirit   is also known as dry cleaning fluid. It's a solvent and is available from hardware shops.

Whiting   is a fine-grade abrasive powder used in cleaning and polishing glass, furniture and polychromate sinks. When mixed with glycerine it can clean most plastics. It's available from hardware shops.

WD-40   stands for Water Displacement, 40th Attempt. It's a high-grade penetrating oil and stops corrosion. It lubricates small areas and can inhibit the presence of some insects.

Woolite   is a mild soap or detergent specifically formulated for delicate fabrics. It is readily available from most supermarkets.

WHAT TO DO ABOUT UNEXPECTED VISITORS

These days, thanks to mobile phones, it's more likely that people will ring before popping over, so you may have 10 minutes to get the place in order. But what can you do if visitors arrive unannounced at the front door and your house has got that lived-in homely look? Here are a few suggestions:

NO WARNING

I keep a cloth impregnated with lavender oil near the front door so that when there are unexpected visitors, I can wipe over the back edges of the door before opening it. The smell is fresh and creates an impression of cleanliness. You could also keep a spray bottle filled with lavender oil and water and give it a squirt before opening the door. It has the same effect. Guide your visitors to the cleanest room and excuse yourself as you make them a cup of tea. In the kitchen, if you don't have a dishwasher, stack any unwashed dishes in a pile because it appears neater, and wipe down any surfaces. You could even place a pair of

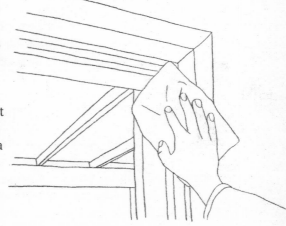

washing-up gloves over the top of the dishes to suggest you were just
about to wash them if you hadn't been interrupted by your visitors!

IF YOU HAVE 10 MINUTES

Just focus on the areas that your guests will see. First, grab your
clutter bucket and gather extraneous items, then put it into a room
you can close off. Stack dishes in the kitchen into a neat pile if you
don't have a dishwasher. Put papers into a neat pile. You'll be amazed
at how much cleaner an area appears if things are neatly ordered
rather than strewn around. Grab a damp cloth and wipe over surfaces.
Throw a tablecloth over the table. Throw a sheet over the washing
basket. Wipe door jambs with a lavender-oil impregnated cloth to give
a fresh smell. Check the toilet is clean. If it's not, give it a quick scrub
with the toilet brush and spray some lavender oil in the air. Quickly
sweep outside the front door – a tidy entrance always makes a great
first impression – and your 10-minute speedclean is done.

Making an Entrance

There's no escaping the fact that the entrance to your house creates that all-important first impression. Make it as open, clean and airy as possible. Nobody wants to walk into a dark, dank cave. It's worth-while standing at the front of your house, taking a good look around, and working out what your entrance says about you. If you don't like the message, then it's time for a revamp! Always make a point of including the area immediately outside and inside your front door in your speedclean; that way you will impress your guests, as well as giving yourself that warm feeling when you come home at this threshold between the outside world and your domestic sanctuary.

If you think your cleaning is slow...

HOW TO CLEAN CARPET FROM *LEE'S PRICELESS RECIPES*, 1817

Take your carpet outside, shake and beat well. Then pack down firmly. Then, with a clean wool flannel cloth, wash over with one quart of bullock's gall mixed with 3 quarts of soft water. Then rub it off with a clean flannel or linen cloth. Very dirty spots should be rubbed with pure bullock's gall. If the carpets are very soiled, rub them with a new broom and grated raw potatoes. For an alternative method, use half a bar of Castile soap, 2 ounces of borax and 2 ounces of washing soda. Boil in half a gallon of water until dissolved. Then add 2 gallons of tepid water. Boil for another 10 minutes. When cold, add half a pint of alcohol. Rub on with a clean piece of woollen flannel.

ASSEMBLE YOUR CLEAN KIT

 Clutter bucket – to transport displaced items; **bicarb** – cleaning agent; **vinegar** – cleaning agent; **water** – cleaning agent; **methylated spirits** – to clean mirrors; **cloth** – (such as an old T-shirt) to wipe and dust surfaces; **straw broom** – to sweep floors and clear cobwebs; **dustpan and brush** – to clear accumulated dirt; **vacuum cleaner** – to vacuum floors; **mop** – to wipe over floors; **bucket** – to hold water or to hold cleaning items; **rubber gloves** – to protect hands and provide grip; **Scotchgard** – to spray over carpet and rugs to protect them from dirt; **hairdryer** – to clean ornaments; **spray bottle** – to fill with vinegar or fragrance.

SPEEDCLEAN OUTSIDE YOUR FRONT DOOR

Remove anything that doesn't belong in this area with a clutter bucket. Then begin clearing any spider webs outside the front door, including around light fittings, with a broom. To deter spiders, wipe the broom head with a little lemon oil before sweeping and it will transfer to surfaces as you clean. Wipe along the door jambs, lock plate and doorknob with the appropriate cleaner. For brass, use a little vinegar on a cloth. For wood, use a little vinegar on a cloth or detergent and water. Dust the door with a dry cloth. If you have furniture on the front garden, clean according to its surface (see page 159). Shake your entrance mat and sweep the path or entranceway with a good straw yard broom. If there's a lot of refuse, collect it in a dustpan and place it straight into the bin. Water any pot plants and remove any dead heads or portions of the plant that have died.

HOW TO MAKE CLEANING SPEEDIER

One of the best ways to speed up your cleaning is to prevent dirt from getting into the house in the first place. That's why a mat placed at the front and back doors of the house is so important. A mat is a bit like a security guard for dirt. I think the best kind of mat is a copra one. If the drainage around your mat is poor, put a rubber-tyre strip mat underneath the copra mat, which will help with ventilation and keep it dry.

> **DID YOU KNOW?** In the pioneer days in Australia, mats were used for wiping dirty shoes and to indicate whether the house was receiving guests. One side of the mat read 'Welcome' and the other side was blank. If the mat was blank, you knew to call at another time.

MATS

The best way to clean a copra mat is to give it a good bash against a wall, then hose the top and bottom. Dry it in the sunshine standing on its edge. Stop your cat or dog from sleeping on the welcome mat by spraying the mat with insecticide.

SPEEDCLEAN INSIDE YOUR FRONT DOOR

Using the same clean kit, remove extraneous items with a clutter bucket and empty any bins. Dust the ceiling and light fittings with a soft nylon broom that has a little lemon oil on it (the oil will transfer to the ceiling and light fittings and deter spiders). Sweep along the walls and tops of cupboards or hallstands.

It's inevitable that you'll get marks on the wall, especially in high traffic areas. Be careful when using proprietary products to clean these marks because most have an alcohol base that can break down the paint surface and leave a bleached shiny spot. Clean your walls every week either with a broom or vacuum cleaner. Put an old T-shirt over the broom head or brush to prevent bristle marks. Some dirty marks will come off using a good pencil eraser. You could also try rolling brown bread into a ball and rubbing it against the wall. If these don't work, try a very diluted solution of sugar soap applied with a cloth. Wring out the cloth tightly before applying. For build-up around light switches, apply vinegar and water sparingly with a sponge. To avoid drip lines, start cleaning from the bottom and work your way up, drying as you go.

> **HINT**
>
> Every time you change a light bulb, clean the other light bulbs with a cloth and they'll shine brighter. To prevent halogen lights corroding, wipe the connection on the bulb with a cloth once a week.

Remove dust and grime from any paintings, wall hangings or wall art. Clean light switches, door jambs and any window sills. Clean any furniture with the appropriate cleaner.

If it's been raining, clear the water in umbrella stands or you'll create a mould farm or a home for frogs!

> **HINT**
>
> Create your own umbrella stand with a spaghetti jar. The bulb at the bottom of the jar is a perfect water collector.
>
> **What to do if you get a water stain on the carpet from umbrellas**
> If you get to the stain immediately, blot as much as possible with a paper towel. A chamois cleaning block is ideal in this situation. If the stain has been there for a while, wipe it with a little glycerine then apply a quality spot remover and use a paper towel to absorb as much moisture as possible.

Wipe the top of the table or hallstand according to its surface. Hallstands often have mirrors which should be cleaned with methylated spirits wrung out on a lint-free cloth, such as an old T-shirt.

HINT

If you don't have room for a hallstand, install some hooks either behind the front door or along the wall to store coats. If you're in a rental property, use removable hooks that wrap over the top of the door. You can also now buy reusable adhesive hooks.

When cleaning picture frames, clean **glass** with methylated spirits and a cloth but be careful not to get methylated spirits around the edges or it could seep into the print. **Polycarbonate** should only be cleaned with a damp cloth. Clean **metal** and **wood** as you would furniture. Clean **plastic** with glycerine.

Clean floors by either vacuuming and/or mopping. To mop, I wrap an old T-shirt that has been dampened with water and vinegar over a broom head, fix it with elastic bands and wipe over the floor. If you have rugs in this space, shake them outside. And remember, rugs and carpet are less likely to absorb stains if sprayed with Scotchgard. You can spray just at the entrance or the whole hallway – wherever there is a high dirt rate – which is particularly useful when it's raining and there's mud around.

DID YOU KNOW? Black mud can be cleaned with detergent and cold water, but if you have red mud, use soap and cold water. Detergent reacts with the iron and manganese oxide in red mud and leaves a rusty or black mark. Soap won't do this because it's saponin-based. Never allow moisture to penetrate the carpet or you'll create further staining from the back of the carpet.

HINT

To freshen dingy carpets, make up a spray bottle containing 1 part bicarb to 3 parts vinegar and 5 parts water. If you like fragrance, add a couple of drops of your favourite essential oil, but avoid fruit oils because the brain associates them with the kitchen. Lightly spray the carpet, don't go overboard and soak it, then sweep it with a T-shirt-covered broom. Sprinkling bicarb on the carpet before vacuuming is a good general carpet freshener, but won't necessarily clean stains. These will have to be spot cleaned.

Water any pot plants, arrange fresh flowers, spray fragrance, if you like using it, or add any froufrou, such as doilies. Empty the clutter bucket, put away the clean kit and update the master list.

STRATEGIES TO MAKE CLEANING SPEEDIER

Light switches are often forgotten about when cleaning. Given the amount of contact they have with dirty fingers, it's a good idea to get into the habit of wiping over them. Whatever you do, never spray cleaning product directly onto them or you could short-circuit the electricity. I dampen a cloth with white vinegar and wipe it over the light switch. Add bicarb to the vinegar cloth if it's particularly dirty.

FLOORS

I like to have a rug or mat inside the front door. If you have carpet, you may have it made from a matching carpet square; just make sure it doesn't have a thick edge that people can trip over. I'd also suggest attaching rubber mesh underneath so it doesn't slip or curl.

You may want to create a space for damp shoes either outside the front door or on the hallstand, if you have one. Use a wooden box or basket and line it with a plastic bag so that water doesn't soak through to the floor and leave puddle marks. Some hallstands have a metal drip tray built into them which is perfect for muddy shoes and umbrellas. Clean them with bicarb and vinegar on a cloth, but if they contain lead, be very careful and always wear rubber gloves when cleaning. Lead, a cumulative poison absorbed into the bloodstream through the skin's pores, can kill.

It's also a good idea to have some storage at the back of the house for dirty shoes and sports gear. A large basket or a small cupboard or even a bucket with a lid should do the trick. It depends on how much sports gear you have. If you can, use a cupboard with good ventilation. And store some bicarb here so that your sports stars can dust inside their shoes before putting them away. Bicarb will help absorb those sweaty smells. Just remember to remove the bicarb before wearing the shoes again.

Shake it out the same way you would if you had sand in your shoes. If the smell from trainers is really overpowering, you may have to do what I did in a share house one time and insist the offending shoes were stored in a plastic dustbin at the back of the garage!

Some people like to keep their sunglasses, scarves, bags and coats on the table or hallstand so they're quickly accessible. But be careful leaving bags and keys here, particularly if you live in the city. I had a friend whose keys were stolen by a thief using a fishing rod through the locked front security door. Rather than just dumping things on the hallstand or table, have a wooden storage box with a lid or a small cupboard. It's just as easy to use, prevents clutter and everything is hidden away and tidy. Make dividers in the box for each family member and clean out the compartments each week as part of the speedclean.

You could also install some hooks in the box or on the inside of the cupboard for keys. Colour code the keys so you don't confuse them.

DID YOU KNOW? Changes in the weather cause locks to expand, contract and corrode. When it's wet or humid, lubricate locks with a graphite puffer or talcum powder. You can use WD-40, but if you have a lot of dust, it can clog up the mechanism; so be careful.

If you tend to dump your post and other stuff near the door, keep a wastepaper basket here as well. That way, unwanted bits and pieces can be thrown out immediately. Because it's at the entrance to your house, make sure it's a stylish bin. Having one here will increase your speed when cleaning.

The entrance to each house will be different and the lifestyle of the people using the house will vary. Shape it to suit your needs, being careful not to overclutter this area. Consider shifting rarely used items to the study or to the back of the house.

FLOWERS AND ORNAMENTS

I know many people like to keep flowers at the entrance to their home, but did you know they die more quickly here because of the draught coming through the door? Potted plants are a much better idea, particularly daisies, because they contain pyrethrum, which deters insects. Select plants with low water needs, such as succulents, although I avoid spiky ones after snagging my stockings several times! Scented herbs are also good because they keep the house smelling fresh when you brush past them, and they come in handy when cooking. Have deep saucers under your pots so water doesn't spill and create more cleaning!

HINT

What to do if you get lily stamens or pollen on the carpet
If the stain has set, damp it with paraffin oil applied with a cotton wool ball. Then damp the stain with methylated spirits applied with a cotton wool ball. Dry with a paper towel before repeating. Do this until the colour is removed. Some pollens will be easy to remove, others will need several attempts. To avoid the problem, remove the stamens before putting the flowers on display. Put a plastic bag over your hand and pull the stamens out into your palm, then wrap the bag over itself and the stamens and throw it in the bin. This way, your hands won't come in contact with the stamens.

HINT

Instead of flowers, create an impression at the entrance to your home with a covered potpourri bowl, rock art, water art, paintings behind glass (to protect them from dust and allow easy cleaning) washable hangings, wind chimes, beautiful shells or pot plants.

The entrance is also a popular area to display ornaments but I don't recommend it because there are higher dust volumes in this part of the house. There's also the danger they could be knocked over in the wind. If you do keep ornaments here, clean them with a hairdryer on the lowest setting and secure them by putting some Blu-tak on the bottom. But only use Blu-tak on non-absorbent surfaces as it will leave an oily stain.

MOTH INFESTATION: Trisha's call to Shannon on radio

Q: 'I'm desperate,' admits Trisha. 'We've got moths in the carpet. We had the insect people in and they said there was nothing they could do. Do you have a solution?'

SOLUTION: In a spray bottle, mix 1 teaspoon of cedar oil, 1 teaspoon of oil of cloves and 1 litre of warm water. Then spray a thin coat of this mixture over the carpet. Repeat every 6–8 weeks, which is the usual breeding cycle of moths.

HINT

This is an area where dog poo can hit
Remove as much of the solids as possible then blot with a paper towel until the carpet is touch dry. Sprinkle bicarb over the area. Then wring out a cloth in vinegar and sponge off the bicarb. If your dog eats commercial food, it will have a high caramel content to colour the food so you'll need to wipe the area with glycerine first. Just apply a small amount of glycerine to a cloth and wipe over the area. Fill a bucket with cold water and enough detergent to create a sudsy mix. Use just the detergent suds, not the water, from the bucket and work them into the stain with a soft nylon brush. Dry it with a chamois cleaning block or use a paper towel to absorb the moisture. When dry, vacuum. If there's any unpleasant odour, repeat this process. An alternative method is to apply cold water and detergent suds with an old toothbrush, using as little water as possible. Then fill the bucket with warm water and detergent and again apply the suds to the stain with an old toothbrush. The reason you use both cold and warm water is because faeces contain proteins and fats. Cold water removes proteins and warm water removes fats. **You must clean in this order or the warm water will set the protein stain!** Dry with a paper towel or chamois cleaning block by standing on it.

CLEANING LIGHTS AND LAMPS

Dust lights and lamps with an old T-shirt for a speedclean.

Light shades made of fabric should be dry cleaned or cleaned with carpet cleaner or brushed with bran and vinegar. Once the carpet cleaner or bran and vinegar is dry, use the brush head on your vacuum cleaner to remove it. Make sure the brush is clean first or you'll create more mess. Glass light-shades should be cleaned in warm water. Clean brass and metal arms with a good quality brass polish – and make sure you don't get cleaning product in the electrical fittings. To cut down on bugs, spray the tops of light shades with surface insecticide.

CLEANING PAINTINGS

Acrylic paintings can be cleaned with a damp cloth. **Water colours** should be cleaned by a professional. To remove residue and dust from **oil paintings**, clean with stale urine, salt and potato. This technique is a guaranteed conversation stopper! Collect 1 litre of female urine and leave it in the sun for a week to reduce to 500 ml. Add 1 tablespoon of salt and 2 table-spoons of grated raw potato. Stir and allow the mixture to sit for 30 minutes. Dampen a cloth in the mixture, wring it out and then wipe gently over the painting. Dampen a clean cloth in water and wipe the painting gently and pat it dry. You can also rub brown bread over the painting to clean it but it can induce mould if the atmosphere is damp, so don't use this technique if you're in a damp, dark spot. For any serious cleaning problems, see a restorer. Never use alcohol-based cleaners such as methylated spirits or turpentine on **gilded frames**. Most gilding is covered with a layer of shellac and alcohol-based cleaners will affect it. Instead, dust the frame with a hairdryer on the cool setting. This should be enough to clean it but if dirt remains, wipe a damp cloth over the frame and then dry it with a soft cloth.

Protect paintings by spraying a cloth with surface insecticide and wipe it over the back of picture frames. Don't touch the painting, just the frames.

STAIRS

Your stairs could be as grand as those in the film *Gone with the Wind* or they could be very plain and functional. No matter how big they are or what their finish is, every corner of every tread must be vacuumed once a week because it's a dust haven. Before vacuuming, run up and down the stairs several times to dislodge as much dust as possible. It's great exercise. Get the kids to do it! Then, if you have pictures in the stairwells, wipe over the frames with a damp cloth. Start cleaning from the top of the stairs and work your way down because dust lifts and drops down. Then vacuum by facing up the stairs, keeping your vacuum cleaner in front of you, and walking backwards down the stairs one step at a time, cleaning each step as you go. That way, your body will stop the vacuum cleaner from tumbling down the stairs and will put less stress on your back. As you vacuum each step, also vacuum between the banister posts with the nozzle or brush

attachment. The brass rods, which hold runners in place, need to be polished with bicarb and vinegar on a cloth or just vinegar if you clean them regularly.

Banisters need to be dusted and polished according to what they're made of. Clean brass with vinegar and water applied with a cloth. Aluminium is cleaned with cold tea applied with a cloth. Clean steel with vinegar and water applied with a cloth. Painted metal or plastic can be wiped with a little detergent and water or vinegar on a cloth. For French polished wood, use beeswax, lavender oil and lemon oil applied with a cloth or you can also use a good non-silicone furniture polish.

> **HINT**
>
> To create the lavender oil, lemon oil and beeswax cleaning cloth, get a microwave-safe bowl. Place a cleaning cloth in the bowl, then add 1 drop of lavender oil, 1 drop of lemon oil and 1 tablespoon of beeswax to the top of the cloth. Warm it in the microwave in 10-second bursts until the beeswax melts. The cloth will be impregnated with the mixture and is ready to use. Store it in a zip-lock plastic bag.

Special attention should be paid to the end of banisters because lots of people grab onto them with their hands and leave messy finger marks. Make sure you remove all the marks. Wipe between the banister posts with a cloth that's been wrung out in water.

Then vacuum underneath the stairs.

YOUNG ARTISTS: Catherine's call to Shannon on radio

Q: 'The kids love painting,' reports Catherine. 'And the other night, they decided to do a school project on the white rug. Help!'

SOLUTION: Put some methylated spirits into a bowl then place the bowl underneath the paint stain, immersing the stained part of the rug into the bowl. Place a glass cover over the top of the stained part of the rug, so the methylated spirits doesn't evaporate. Soak until the paint is removed. Then rinse in water and dry in the sun.

If the stairs are wooden, vacuum and then wipe with a mop. I prefer to use a broom, which has its broom head wrapped in an old T-shirt dampened with vinegar and secured with an elastic band.

HINT

To speed up polishing, instead of a duster, use a pair of old cotton socks over your hands.

TO MAKE CLEANING SPEEDIER

Speed up your cleaning by making sure extension cords are long enough before you start vacuuming. How many times have you nudged into a corner thinking the cord would just make it and then lost power? You then have to walk all the way back to the power point, add an extension cord and resume your cleaning. It's a time waster! So sort that out before starting the job. I also use a protector to cover the joins of extension cords so they don't scratch the surface of things.

If your stairs are carpeted, make sure the carpet is tight and well fitted so that dust havens aren't created.

Clean the back entrance of the house in the same way as the
front entrance.

LINEN CUPBOARD

Linen cupboards can be located in various spots in a house.
Many are situated at the end of the front hallway or on landings.
    I don't feel at home unless my linen cupboard is sorted.
Whenever I move house, it's the first thing I arrange. It also means
a pretty tablecloth is ready to use if people suddenly pop over.
You may not have time to polish a table, but you can always
throw a tablecloth over it!

The linen cupboard should be sorted by having items most
used at eye level, those least used on higher levels and items for
children, such as towels, on lower levels. Make sure there's
nothing dangerous on the lower, child-accessible levels.

Speed your cleaning by storing linen according to the room it's
used in. That way, when you're cleaning a particular room, you
can easily grab one pile of linen rather than sorting through
several shelves. If you only have a limited amount of storage
space, have the linen piled from bottom to top, but group it
according to the room it's used in. If you have items stored for a
long time, wrap them in acid-free tissue paper to stop them
from going yellow. Acid-free tissue paper is available from art
supply shops, picture framers and sometimes from dry cleaners.

HINT

If an item has gone yellow, it's generally because of soap residue. To repair cotton items, soak them in **Napisan**. For silk, hand wash in 60 ml of lemon juice added to a nappy-sized bucket of blood-heat water, then dry in the sun. For vintage items, use 2 teaspoons of soap flakes, 60 ml of white vinegar added to a bucket of blood-heat water, rinse then dry.

Bugs love linen, so keep bath salts and fragrant soaps in the linen cupboard to deter them. The salts and soaps will leave a lovely scent on your linen. Also use scented paper liners on the shelves, which you can make yourself, as explained on page 81. Never store medicine in this cupboard because the linen will absorb the smell. Even Band-Aids have an odour that will be absorbed by the linen.

Cleaning the linen press is a spring/autumn cleaning job. Remove all the linen (I have a trolley with two large shelves on which I pile the contents of the linen press), then vacuum the shelves of the linen press. Shake each item and refold before returning it to its spot in the linen press.

DAILY CHECKLIST FOR ENTRANCE

· **empty bin**
· **tidy hallstand**

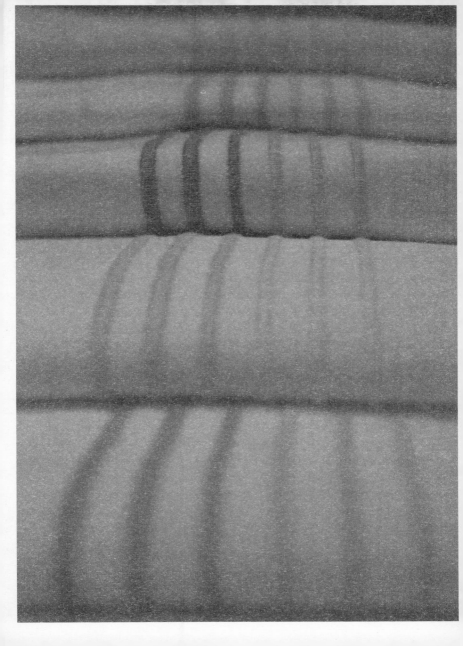

Lounge, Dining, Family Rooms and Study

For many people, there's not a lot of lounging going on in the lounge. In some homes, this area is converted into a playroom for children with toys such as racing car tracks and doll's houses placed smack bang in the middle of the room. Other houses combine all the communal areas of the home – the lounge, dining and family rooms – into a grand living space. And yet other houses have separate lounge and dining rooms, formal spaces that are reserved for special occasions, which may also be the show-off rooms – the places where guests are likely to spend their time. Whatever your arrangement, the cleaning process is similar. Tailor these general instructions to your individual needs!

If you think your cleaning is slow...

HOW TO CLEAN CARPET FROM *LEE'S PRICELESS RECIPES*, 1817

If you have dark-coloured carpet, you can revive its colour. Grate two potatoes, cover them in hot water, leave for 2 hours then strain. Dip a brush into the liquid and wipe it over the carpet. The colour should brighten. Don't use this on light carpets.

ASSEMBLE THE CLEAN KIT

Clutter bucket – to transport displaced items; **bicarb** – cleaning agent; **white vinegar** – cleaning agent; **methylated spirits** – to clean mirrors and entertainment systems; **furniture polish** – to polish furniture; **beeswax, lavender oil, lemon oil** – combined to make furniture polish; **cloth** – to wipe over surfaces; **dusters** – to clear dust; **paper towel** – to absorb water and polish; **insecticide spray** –

to deter insects; **spray bottle** – to hold vinegar and water; **hairdryer** – to clean ornaments; **small soft paintbrush** – to clean ornaments.

LOUNGE SPEEDCLEAN

Begin with your clutter bucket, putting in it anything that doesn't belong in the lounge. Place it outside the lounge. Add a little lemon oil to a soft broom head or a long-handled duster and dust the ceiling and light fittings – the lemon oil will transfer to the dusted surface and inhibit spiders. Then dust the walls with a broom covered in an old T-shirt. Wipe down all paintings, picture frames or wall art, especially along the tops of frames. Wipe light switches and power points with vinegar on a cloth. Wipe door jambs with either vinegar or detergent and water on a cloth adding lavender oil for fragrance. Dust over window sills.

> **HINT**
>
> There is a knack to cleaning window sills. Use the fine nozzle or brush head on the vacuum cleaner and vacuum all the dust. Wipe over with a cloth that's been wrung out in water. If there's any build-up of grime in the corners, wrap a cloth that's been wrung out in water over a butter knife and reach into the corners. You can clean sashes in the same way. The window action will work better if it's kept clean.

Wipe all surfaces including the coffee table with the appropriate cleaner (see pages 54–59 for details on how to clean surfaces). I advise against using silicone-based cleaners as silicone builds up each time you use it, trapping dirt between the layers and because there's no solvent for it, you can't release that dirt! To clean laminate, use equal parts white vinegar and water on a cloth.

Clean glass tabletops with methylated spirits and a cloth, then wipe the glass with a paper towel until it squeaks. Never use furniture polish on glass and see a restorer for scratches. Perspex tables can only be cleaned with washing-up liquid and water. Never use abrasives on perspex or it will mark (proprietary window cleaners are abrasive).

Don't forget to wipe along shelves. Anything that's a dust magnet, such as knick knacks, bric-a-brac or ephemera needs to be wiped with a cloth that has been tightly wrung out in water.

HINTS FOR BLOKES: Because most men think visually, if they can't see it, they won't clean it. If dust and dirt is out of sight, before you start cleaning, use a three-step ladder to see where things need to be cleaned.

Dust should be blown off fragile ornaments with a hairdryer on a low setting. Loosen any tough spots with a small soft paint-brush then use the hairdryer. See pages 58–59 for detailed information on caring for ornaments.

If your fireplace is operational, clean it after each use. To clean the surrounds, simply dust the area with a soft clean cloth. Clean the mantelpiece according to what it's made of. Use diluted vinegar to clean marble, then rinse with clean water. Wood can be cleaned with a little washing-up liquid, water and an old pair of stockings scrunched into a ball. If there is smoke or soot staining, try cleaning with vinegar and an old pair of pantyhose first. If that doesn't work, collect some of the ash from the fireplace, mix with water to make a slurry, then wipe over the area. Allow it to dry then rub off with an old pair of pantyhose. To clean the inside cavity of the fireplace, hire a chimney sweep when you do your spring clean.

Next, sprinkle a small amount of bicarb over the carpet, sofas and soft furnishings. Roughly pat the bicarb through the soft furnishings with your hands to both deodorise and clean any light soil marks. Then vacuum the soft furnishings and the floor. Make sure you remove the cushions on the sofa and chairs and vacuum underneath them.

If you spill something on the sofa, work out what the stain is made of, then use its solvent. Remove protein stains with cold water and soap suds, remove fats with warm water and detergent suds, remove chemicals with their solvent. You can identify protein stains because they have a dark edging around the stain. Carbohydrate stains are evenly coloured across the stain. (See pages 184–91 for more on stains.)

If there are any spider webs around the sofa, remove them and wipe lemon oil on the underside of the sofa. Spiders hate lemon oil and will stay away.

Don't forget to clean bookshelves with the brush head attachment on the vacuum cleaner. Vacuum curtains, pelmets and picture rails with the brush head attachment. Before using the brush head attachment, make sure it's clean. To clean it, wash in water and dry in the sunshine.

Vacuum floors and if it's a hard floor, wipe over with a cloth that's been wrung out in vinegar.

Replace items such as doilies and tissues and fluff cushions. Have a small bowl of bicarb and essential oil for fragrance. Empty the clutter bucket then put away your clean kit and top up your master list.

UNWANTED GUESTS: Helen's call to Shannon on radio

Q: INCIDENT: 'We recently had our linen-blend sofa cleaned,' says Helen. 'And then we found some dead silverfish. What can we do?'

SOLUTION: The best way to deter silverfish is with whole cloves. Scatter them at the back of and underneath the sofa.

DINING ROOM SPEEDCLEAN

Dining areas are incredibly diverse, ranging from the formal to the chaotic. Use the same speedcleaning technique as for the lounge.

If you think your cleaning is slow...

HOW TO CLEAN MAHOGANY FROM *LEE'S PRICELESS RECIPES*, 1817

Take 1 quart of proof alcohol. Cut therein all the gum shellac it will take. Add 2 ounces of Venice turpentine and colouring to suit. This makes a beautiful polish and will wear for years.

TABLES

If you have a valuable wooden dining table, I strongly suggest using a table protector to guard against scratches. Use heat-resistant placemats and have extra mats for the centre of the table when serving. Using tablecloths will cut down on mess and speed your cleaning.

DID YOU KNOW? Mixing beeswax, lavender oil and lemon oil on a cloth is a great wood cleaner. Antique shops often use this combination (see page 43 for recipe).

WHAT IS FRENCH POLISH?

French polish is created by layering very thin coatings of shellac either on wood or papier-mâché. Clean it with a non-silicone-based furniture polish. Try not to use water near French polish because it will whiten the surface.

To repair a heat mark on a table

Heat marks appear as a white ring on your table. To repair a French polish finish, use beeswax applied with a piece of lemon peel. If the table is very damaged, use a mixture of 1 part bicarb and 1 part olive oil, paint it onto the mark, leave for a few minutes, then polish it off with a cloth. Polish normally.

Be very careful with polyurethane surfaces because if you scratch them, you'll have to reseal them. If you do scratch the surface of polyurethane, wipe it with **Brasso** in the direction of the grain. The mark will become worse before it gets better. **Brasso** works because it partially melts polyurethane. If the scratch has penetrated through to the wood, you'll have to reseal the area which is a big job. If this is the case, seek the advice of a professional.

If heat has bubbled the surface, for French polish, see a restorer. For a polyurethane finish, fill a syringe with 1 part **Aquadhere** to 20 parts water. The mixture should be the consistency of runny cream. Inject a small quantity into the centre of the bubble then press down. Place a weight, such as a heavy book, on it while it dries, using a piece of cling film to protect the underside of the book.

DID YOU KNOW? Most raw timbers are best treated with teak oil or Sheraton oil, which feed the timber surfaces.

CHAIRS

Don't forget to wipe chairs because they are great dust collectors – and don't forget to clean the legs as well.

Vinyl   Clean vinyl with vinegar and water mixture then rinse with a damp cloth.

Fabric   Wash loose fabric covers or removable cushions regularly, either by hand or in the washing machine. If you can, have two sets of covers so you can replace them immediately. If you like, use different colours to change the whole of the dining area. Upholstered chairs should be vacuumed or brushed thoroughly with a lint- or clothes-brush. If they're stained, mix bran and white vinegar until it forms clumps and rub it over the stain. Leave to dry, then vacuum.

Leather   Leather should be treated with leather dew. For scratches, if the leather is brown, rub a cut walnut along the scratch. For other colours, use shoe cream along the scratch.

Wood   Wood should be cleaned with a small amount of cider vinegar, water and a damp cloth. Shellac or French polish should be cleaned with a good non-silicone furniture polish.

Plastic   Plastic should be cleaned with a cloth wrung out in water. For stubborn stains, use washing-up liquid applied with a cloth. Minor scratches can be treated with a small amount of glycerine on a cloth.

Stainless steel   The best way to clean stainless steel is with bicarb and vinegar. Mix them together on a sponge and wipe over the chair. Then wipe with a cloth that's been wrung out in water. For scratches, apply a dab of Gumption to a sponge and wipe over the scratch. Then apply bicarb and vinegar and clean with a cloth.

Chrome   Clean chrome with a cloth and a little detergent and water or vinegar.

MIRRORS

If you have mirrors in this room, clean them with a lint-free cloth dampened with methylated spirits and wrung out.

> **HINT**
>
> Place mirrors high enough on the wall so that they can be tilted. Mirrors should never be flat but rather sit with a 10 per cent tilt forward. A tilted mirror also speeds cleaning because not as much dust will sit on top of the mirror's edge – it also makes your legs look thinner!

> **HINT**
>
> **If you drop candle wax on carpet or fabric**
> Put ice on the wax to harden it then scrape as much away as possible with a blunt knife. Wedge a metal comb underneath the wax and put a paper towel on top of the wax, then use a hairdryer over it. The paper towel will absorb the wax. Repeat until all the wax is removed. Never use an iron on carpet as it can char natural fibres or melt synthetic fibres.

ORNAMENTS

Brass should be cleaned using a proprietary cleaner or my choice of cleaner, bicarb and vinegar. If you're coating it, use shellac rather than brass coat because it can be removed more easily. Be aware that brass will tarnish even after being coated, but the coating will help it last a little longer.

Bronze can be cleaned with a damp soapy cloth but never rub bronze or you'll remove the patina.

China should be dusted with a hairdryer on a low setting and use a small paintbrush for those difficult-to-reach areas. Wash every six months in blood-heat water and dry thoroughly with a hairdryer. If very dirty, add a little detergent to the water except if the item has non-china elements, such as lace or paper. Never soak china.

Clay should be vacuumed and dusted regularly. Never soak because clay absorbs moisture. If you wash, do so quickly and dry thoroughly so you don't lift the glaze.

Cloisonné is enamel fused into small wire pockets on the outside of a bronze, brass or copper vessel. Clean it with vinegar and water. Never use soaps because it will tarnish.

Embroidery, where possible, should be kept out of direct sunlight. Keep it covered and inside cabinets. Hand wash gently if it's colourfast. If not, take it to a restorer or a good dry cleaner.

Ephemera should be kept as flat as possible under glass or in cabinets. Spray fabric with surface insecticide spray to keep bugs away.

Fabrics can be treated as you would your best table linen. Keep them well dusted and, where possible, vacuum.

Ivory can be cleaned with sweet almond oil applied with a cloth.

Lace should be hand washed in pure soap and rinsed very well. Glue medical gauze underneath a hole to hold it until you're ready to repair it properly. Embroider over the gauze in the same pattern as the lace, trimming away any excess gauze when you have finished.

Paper must be kept dust free and away from direct sunlight. Wash carefully with a slightly damp cloth. Just dab rather than wipe the paper. If in doubt, use a restorer or conservator.

Silver can be cleaned with a proprietary cleaner or bicarb soda and vinegar. Polish with bran.

Tinware can be wiped with warm soapy water and dried thoroughly with a rag dampened with sewing machine oil. This will prevent rust. If tin does rust, apply **WD-40** with a cloth. To stop bugs eating paper labels on tinware, wipe the labels with a damp tea bag.

Wood, if it's sealed, can be cleaned using a good silicone-free furniture polish. If it's unsealed, clean with furniture oil.

DID YOU KNOW? If there's heavy plant matter stuck in the base of a vase, use bicarb and vinegar. If that doesn't work, add coarse salt and vinegar and shake. Then rinse and allow to dry.

To speed your cleaning, keep anything that collects dust under a shelf. The shelf will collect the dust rather than the item.

If you have rugs, take them outside, hang them over the clothesline and whack them with a heavy item such as a tennis racquet, cricket bat or golf club, although be careful not to bend it! Vacuum the room.

BAD MARKS: Ali's call to Shannon on radio

Q: INCIDENT: 'You've got to help me!' pleads Ali. 'I've got permanent marker on my brown nylon carpet and it looks awful.'

SOLUTION: This is a difficult problem to fix. Try to remove the marker with egg white. Paint egg white over the permanent marker stain, leave it to dry then brush the egg white away with your fingers. The permanent marker should adhere to the egg white. Unfortunately, you will still have a slight shadow but the stain will be much improved.

FAMILY ROOM SPEEDCLEAN

Use the same speedcleaning technique as for the lounge.

STRATEGIES TO MAKE CLEANING SPEEDIER

The family room is often a traffic way from one room to another. If this is the case at your house, create a deliberate walkway. It's much easier to focus on cleaning a specific part of the room. I place a rug over the walkway or spray it with Scotchgard to add another layer of protection from all those feet stomping through the room. Re-Scotchgard every three months or when the carpet is shampooed. You only need to spray a very thin layer.

> **HINT**
>
> If yours is a house with four-legged friends, get rid of fur and hair by putting on disposable rubber gloves, then wash your gloved hands with soap and water, making sure you remove the powder from the gloves (disposable rubber gloves are stored with talcum powder to stop them from perishing). Shake your gloved hands dry and drag them over the fur and hair on the sofa. This also works for removing excess hair from the dog or cat! The rubber in the gloves draws the fur away because the gloves are statically charged when they've been washed and dried. Bath your animal regularly.

Be aware of the room's breezeways. In summer, arrange the room so that cool air can flow through. In winter, however, you're aiming to retain heat. So rearrange the room accordingly.

As with other rooms, deal with stains as quickly as possible. If you spill something on the carpet, work out what the stain is made of then use its solvent. The most important thing is not to get moisture on the carpet because it will penetrate the backing and make it worse. Be very sparing with water. See pages 189–91 for a comprehensive guide.

ENTERTAINMENT SYSTEMS

Television screens, plasma and LCD screens and the exterior of most entertainment systems can be cleaned with 1 part methylated spirits to 4 parts water applied with a lint-free cloth, such as an old T-shirt. If you prefer, proprietary brand equipment cleaners that are antistatic are also available. Just make sure you don't use detergent because it will leave smear marks on these surfaces. Wipe the back of all electrics with a cloth sprayed with surface insecticide spray to keep insects away.

Have a designated spot for remote controls, which seem to be multiplying. Clean them with a damp cloth. If gunk has accumulated between the buttons, clean between them with a cotton bud. If yours tend to go missing, attach them to the coffee table with a Velcro strip and retractable cords.

HINT

HINTS FOR BLOKES: Electronic equipment works better when the vents are clean. Dust them regularly and make sure electronic equipment is kept clean the right way! Never use turpentine on plastics because it will melt!

HINT

Don't keep pot plants near electrical equipment as the plants don't respond well to magnetic fields – and electricity and water don't mix!

BOOKS

Many books are susceptible to UV rays so try to keep them in a shaded area. If your books are discoloured at the top of the page, it means they were cut at too hot a level on cheap paper. You may also find yellowing on either side of photographic paper, which means it's not acid-free. To prevent damp in your books, keep silicone crystals nearby. One bag per shelf should be enough. Doing this will also cut down on cleaning because damp books collect more dust than dry books. If possible, have a shelf over the top of books to collect dust. Vacuum once a week.

DID YOU KNOW? If you get grease on a book, cover the spot above and underneath with blotting paper and iron over it with a warm iron. If the stain remains, wipe two pieces of blotting paper with a little detergent, place them above and underneath the stain then press the page firmly with a very cool iron. It's the pressure, not the heat, that shifts the remaining oil.

AIR CONDITIONERS, FANS AND HEATERS

Be careful with air conditioners. I'm a fuss-pot because I know how easy it is for nasties to breed in them. The main thing is to make sure that the air intake is clean. Remove and clean the filter according to the manufacturer's instructions. Some need to be flushed with water and dried in the sunshine. Others just need to have the dust removed from them. If you do this once a week, it won't become a chore. When you wipe the air conditioner, add lavender oil to the cloth to both scent the room and deter insects. Change air conditioner pipes once a year.

Fans collect dust when they move because they create a static charge. Because dust is so light and oppositely charged, it's attracted to the fan blades and collects grease and makes a horrible mess. If you don't clean fan blades regularly, they'll accumulate an absorbent felt of dust that will go furry. Clean them with either a feather or fabric duster. If your fan is in a sealed unit, unscrew the cover and dust the fan blades. It will work more efficiently and won't spread dust.

Heaters are more efficient if they're dust-free, clean and shiny. Clean and polish reflector plates at the back of the heater with bicarb and vinegar. This will also get rid of rust. Wipe the heating filaments with methylated spirits **but don't turn the heater on until it's dried out completely because methylated spirits is highly flammable**. If you have a gas or paraffin heater, place a saucepan of water beside the heater to absorb the fumes. Add a slice of onion to the water with a paraffin heater.

PIANOS

Most pianos are made of wood and are best cared for with a good silicone-free furniture polish. Piano keys can be made of plastic, ivory or ivorite. You can tell which is which by the lines in the keys. Plastic keys have no lines, ivory has slightly uneven lines and ivorite keys have even lines. Clean plastic keys with glycerine. Ivory keys can be cleaned with sweet almond oil or by rubbing on alcohol then sweet almond oil. If the keys are really dirty, use a small quantity of tooth-paste mixed with water and apply carefully with a cotton bud, then polish off with a cloth. Apply a small quantity of sweet almond oil that will protect the ivory from cracking. Ivorite is cleaned with methylated spirits on a cloth.

Do you remember that experiment at school when you rubbed your hair with a plastic comb then watched as dust was attracted to the plastic? This is the operation of positive and negative ions. Positive ions are created when inorganic materials rub together or against organic materials. In a home, it means furniture attracts dust and becomes statically charged. It tends to happen in those homes with lots of loved clutter. If this is the case at your home, hire a negative ion generator from the hardware shop. Leave the machine on for 1 hour to restore the ion balance. There should be a slightly higher proportion of negative to positive ions to be comfortable. You'll know when you need one if you're accumulating more dust in a week than you can clean.

IN THE DARK: Janet's call to Shannon on radio

Q: INCIDENT: 'We recently had a powercut and had to resort to using candles,' says Janet. 'But my son accidentally knocked over one of the candles and now there's red wax all over a tapestry chair. Can it be fixed?'

SOLUTION: Try and remove as much wax as possible by delicately prising it away with a plastic knife or wooden ice-block stick. For any remaining wax, place some paper towel over it, then apply heat from a hairdryer. The wax should be absorbed by the paper towel. Keep replacing the paper towel until all the wax is removed. To remove the red colouring, use sunlight. Put the chair outside in the sun and, except for the waxed area, cover it. The staining will fade in sunlight. If you can't put the chair in the sun, hire an ultraviolet light, cover the non-stained part of the chair with an old sheet or towel then aim the light over the stained area. Check it every 2 hours until the stain has gone.

STUDY

Every home should have a study or an office, even if it's just a chair and a cupboard. Having one designated spot for papers and documents speeds up your cleaning because you're less likely to have them strewn around the house. I also try to keep my pens and pencils in this spot, although my daughter constantly moves them all around the house. If you keep them in one spot, you minimise ink stains and can always find a pen when you need one. Another way to minimise ink stains is to do what a friend of mine did and ban permanent markers in the house until the children turn five.

> **HINT**
>
> **To remove ink stains**
> On soft furnishings – apply rotten milk solids until the ink bleeds into it. Then clean with a little soap and water. To rot milk, simply leave some full-cream milk in the sun until it goes lumpy. The time it takes for the milk to go off will vary, and it will smell off before it goes off. You must wait until the mixture is lumpy before using. For hard surfaces, apply dry cleaning fluid/white spirit with a cloth and rub straight off with another cloth.

Speedcleaning for the study is the same as for the lounge.

There are many ways to organise your papers, family photographs, bills, letters and documents. Many people use a filing cabinet to organise these items. Others have trays and some people find that old shoe boxes do the job. You could even recycle old cereal boxes for storage but spray them with insecticide first because bugs are attracted to cardboard. Documents need to be kept in a safe spot, and be easily accessible in case of fire or flood. Sort your documents by subject and keep them together in a manila folder. Then order them alphabetically. These days, many people store files electronically, which is fine, but any documents should be backed up. Computer files can be copied onto a memory stick or CD. You could even consider making a copy onto paper or in your computer of all the phone numbers you keep stored in your mobile phone. They're easy to lose and it's time consuming to collect numbers again.

DID YOU KNOW? To find the edge on sticky tape, put talcum powder on your finger and run it around the sticky tape. The edge will go white.

I sort my bills and store them vertically with removable hooks. Each hook keeps a different bill. When the bill is paid, I staple the receipt to it or write the receipt number on it so I can see at a glance which bills have been paid and which ones need to be paid. Having papers hanging vertically means they don't collect dust and don't take

up much room – and it's easier to sort through a stack of vertical papers than a pile on a table. One thing to be careful of is receipts on paper that fades – keep them out of sunlight.

TELEPHONE

I clean the phone with a small amount of white vinegar and water on a cloth. You could also use a little glycerine on a cloth. For the area between the buttons, which is difficult to access, use a cotton bud dipped in white vinegar or glycerine. Never use alcohol-based chemicals or eucalyptus oil to clean the phone because they could melt plastics. Don't forget to clean the phone cord. Start at the receiver, cover the cord with your cleaning cloth and pinch it between your finger and thumb. Then pull the cloth all the way to the end of the cord.

COMPUTER

There are a couple of ways to clean the computer. First, make sure the computer is off. Specialised cleaners are available, but I don't think they're necessary.

For light cleans, use a cloth tightly wrung out in water. Never use a wet cloth because the ports can corrode – and don't even approach the ports with a damp cloth!

For dirty surfaces, apply some antistatic CD spray to a cloth and wipe it over all the surfaces, including the venting hole. Never spray anything directly onto a computer. It's fine to use your vacuum cleaner to get at dirt outside the computer but never use it inside the computer because it creates static electricity and could ruin it. You can vacuum the vent holes.

As for cleaning keyboards, so many people eat near them that it's not unusual for crumbs to lodge under the keys. You can turn it upside down and gently shake it, use your vacuum cleaner or compressed air in a can applied through a nozzle. I use my airbrush compressor. To clean keyboard keys, use cotton buds dampened with a little methylated spirits or water.

To deter bugs, spray surface insecticide spray on a rag and wipe the back of the computer with it. Make sure you keep computers well ventilated by placing them at least 10 cm away from any wall.

MOUSE

You know it's time to clean the mouse when it becomes sticky and hard to move. To clean the inside, turn it over and twist the back cover off the ball. Take the ball out and wipe it with a cloth wrung out in water. Never use chemicals on it. Dampen, but don't wet, a cotton bud with methylated spirits and clean the inside cavity of the mouse including the rollers. When you've removed as much dirt as possible, carefully blow into the hole to make sure all the excess dust comes out. Put the ball back in and attach the back cover. To clean the underside of the mouse, dip a cotton bud in methylated spirits and wipe the slide points that make contact with the mat. Dry it upside down. Give the mouse mat and the cord a wipe with methylated spirits to get rid of skin-cell and sweat build-up.

FAX

Clean the outside of a fax with a cloth wrung out in warm water. Rubber rollers should be cleaned with a little methylated spirits applied with a cotton bud, then cleaned again with a lint-free cloth wrung out in water, which will remove the fibres from the cotton bud.

DID YOU KNOW? If you spill toner, clean it by lightly dampening a bar of soap with water then dab it on the spill. The toner fragments will stick to the soap as though it were sticky tape. Rinse the bar of soap and repeat this process until you've removed as much as possible, then apply rotten milk solids to the remaining stain. Once all the toner ink is absorbed, remove the rotten milk with soap and a little water on a cloth.

PHOTOCOPIER

The photocopier is cleaned in the same way as the fax. Clean the glass with methylated spirits applied with a lint-free cloth. Clean around the buttons with methylated spirits and a cotton bud. Toner can be cleaned from carpet with rotten milk as described on page 69. For excess toner on the photocopier, put on rubber gloves and use a damp cloth to wipe away the toner. Put the cloth into a plastic bag and throw out as it will stain anything it touches. For mechanical repairs, consult a professional.

DAILY CHECKLIST FOR LOUNGE, DINING AND FAMILY ROOMS AND STUDY

· put away projects
· sort mail
· collect any crumbs
· empty bin

The Bedroom

It's very easy for the bedroom to become a clutter zone. Maybe it's because clothes are put on and taken off here, contents of pockets are removed here, make-up is put on here and jewellery is stored here. There are lots of bits and pieces. It's why the rule of 'a place for everything' is paramount. Jennifer's father delights in telling the story of when she was about three years old, he'd come home from a long day at the office, collapsed into a chair and taken his shoes off. She firmly pronounced that 'your shoes should be either on your feet or in the cupboard, not on the floor'. Intuitive speedcleaning!

If you think your cleaning is slow...

THE MAGIC ANNIHILATOR FROM *LEE'S PRICELESS RECIPES*, 1817

To make one gross of 8 ounce bottles, use 1 gallon of aqua ammonia, 8 gallons of soft water, 3 pounds of white Castile soap and 6 ounces of salt petre. Shave soap, add water, boil until soap has dissolved. Allow to go cold, then add the salt petre slowly stirring thoroughly until dissolved. Now strain. Let the suds settle, skim off the dry suds, add ammonia. Bottle and cork it at once. It will remove all kinds of grease and oil spots from every variety of wearing apparel without injury to the finest silks or laces. It will shampoo like a charm, raising a lather in proportion to the amount of dandruff and grease in your hair. It will clean doorknobs.
It will strip paint from a board. It can't be beaten!

ASSEMBLE THE CLEAN KIT

Clutter bucket – to transport displaced items; **clothes' basket** – to transport dirty clothes to the laundry; **spray bottle** – to hold either vinegar or water; **vacuum cleaner** – to vacuum floors and window sills; **damp cloth** – to wipe over surfaces; **dry cloth** – to wipe over surfaces; **furniture polish cloth** – to wipe over wooden furniture; **detergent** – cleaning agent; **beeswax** – to polish; **lemon peel** – to apply beeswax and deter spiders; **methylated spirits** – to clean mirrors and windows; **lavender oil** – fragrance; **elastic bands** – to secure old T-shirts to broom heads; **broom** – to clean floors and walls; **paper towel** – to wipe over surfaces; **old T-shirt** – to use as a cleaning cloth; **rags** – to use as cleaning cloths.

SPEEDCLEAN

With your clutter bucket, clear anything from the room that doesn't belong there. Then strip the sheets from the bed, collect dirty clothes and leave them in a basket outside the door of the bedroom – you'll sort them later in the laundry. Dust the ceiling and light fittings with a soft broom or long-handled duster, then dust the walls and paintings, especially along the tops of frames or wall art. Wipe light switches and power points with white vinegar on a cloth. Wipe door jambs with either white vinegar or detergent and water on a cloth adding lavender oil for fragrance. Don't forget window sills because these are a dust-collecting zone. If a window sill is really grimy, use a small amount of detergent on a damp cloth.

DID YOU KNOW? To remove spider webs, attach an old T-shirt or rag to the wand of your vacuum tube and secure it with an elastic band. Then vacuum the spider webs. Using the rag means the sticky webs will land there rather than get stuck inside the vacuum tube.

How to remove a spider without using insecticide

Find an old ice-cream or takeaway container with a lid. Put the container over the top of the spider then slide the lid underneath so you capture the spider. Then either take the spider outside or flush it down the toilet. If the spider is out of reach, use the bristles of a broom to reach the spider. If the spider's eyes are facing the bristles, it will climb onto them. If not, it will run away. Allow the spider to climb onto the bristles, then bring the broom down to the floor and put the container over the top of the spider. Slide the lid underneath so that the spider is contained. Release the spider outside or flush it down the toilet.

Remove items, such as the clock radio, tissue boxes and lamps, from bedside tables and chests of drawers. Wipe all surfaces with a cloth tightly wrung out in water, working from the top of the room down. I prefer this to dusting with a dry cloth because it cleans better and traps the dust rather than fluffing it around the room. Polish furniture according to the type of finish it has. For wooden surfaces, use a good non-silicone furniture polish with a drop of lavender oil for scent. For laminate finishes, just use a cloth tightly wrung out in water. Then replace items, cleaning them with a damp cloth as you return them.

> If you've left a glass of water on the wooden bedside table
> and it's made a water mark, use beeswax applied with
> lemon peel. To prevent the problem, use a drink coaster.

Don't forget to wipe a damp cloth over the tops of wardrobes.
The dust that gathers here eventually makes its way around the
room so it's important to clean here too. If you have a fan in
the room, clean it as part of the speedclean (see page 75).

> If paper becomes stuck to a surface, remove it with a little
> sweet almond oil or any other soft oil. Wipe over it with a
> rolled-up stocking.

Clean mirrors with methylated spirits and a lint-free cloth, such as
an old T-shirt. Dip the cloth in methylated spirits, wring it out
tightly, then wipe it over the mirror. It shouldn't smear, but if it
does, rub it with a paper towel. Don't use paper towel to clean
because methylated spirits will break the paper down and leave
furry bits on your mirror.

Dust the top and front surface of standing photo frames. Clear
jewellery away and wipe dishes.

Vacuum and mop the floor if you have an uncarpeted
bedroom. Shake rugs outside, return them to their position and
vacuum them. Remake the bed with nice fresh sheets, which is
like a full stop for the room. The last thing to do is fluff your
pillows before putting on clean pillowcases.

DAILY: If you have a rubbish bin, clean it out each day.

Empty out the clutter bucket and take the washing to the washing machine. Add fragrance if you like. I mix my own using 2 drops of detergent and 5 drops of lavender oil in a spray bottle of water. You can also use tea tree oil or any of the floral essential oils. Many people like what I call froufrou, or frilly bits, such as doilies. Add to your taste. Make any additions to the master list.

STRATEGIES TO MAKE CLEANING SPEEDIER

Bedrooms become untidy for three main reasons: clothes, shoes and papers. It's easy to create a system to deal with these.

DAILY: As soon as you remove your dirty clothes, put them straight into a laundry basket. For clothes you'll wear again, get into the habit of putting them away in the wardrobe, not leaving them on the floor or letting them pile up on a chair. In fact, if you hang clothes while they're still warm, they won't need ironing because the heat will iron out the creases. If there are any stains, deal with them as soon as you can. They're harder to clean once they've set.

If there's mending to do, such as sewing a hem or replacing a button, do this before you wash. If you don't, the job will become larger. I have a dedicated sewing basket and mend during the evening while watching TV. If you don't mend garments yourself, create a pile to take to a professional. Mending services are often available at laundrettes and dry cleaners and can sometimes be found right next door to shops that sell suits.

HINTS FOR BLOKES: Men often drop their clothes on the floor. The way my husband manages to avoid this is to use a very contemporary and stylish valet stand. It's got a small shelf for socks, a rack for suits and places to keep keys and bits and pieces. It doesn't take up a lot of room and there's a place for everything, even a laundry bag at the bottom for dirty socks.

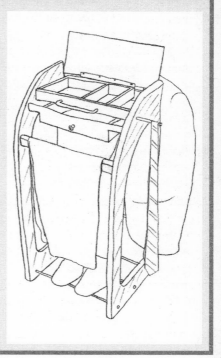

Deal with shoes in a similar way to clothes: as soon as you take them off, put them away in their designated spot in the wardrobe. If they need to be cleaned put them in the laundry.

For strategies on how to deal with papers, see Study on page 66.

You'll also save on cleaning time if the bedroom is arranged to maximise airflow. To achieve this, put the bed either between the window and door or between two windows. This allows air to flow across the bed and stops mould growing and that dank,

mildewy smell. It helps
keep the air dry. Dust sticks
to damp surfaces more
easily than dry ones. If you
have room under your
bed, use it for storage. To
cut back on cleaning, use
storage containers with lids
to prevent dust getting in
under the bed. It means
less vacuuming and is
another way of saving on
cleaning time.

WARDROBES

Stand wardrobes at least
10 cm from the wall so that
air can circulate. If you
have more than one wardrobe, stand them as far apart as
possible to maximise air circulation. If this isn't possible, stand
them right next to each other so you don't create difficult-to-
access dust corridors. Make sure wardrobe doors can be
opened completely so you can easily reach inside.

Save time in your bedroom by organising your wardrobe with
a system so that clothes are easier to find. You might organise
your clothes by size, style, colour, how heavy they are or season.
Hang your wardrobe in sections putting similar types of clothes
together. All your shirts should be together, for example. Then
order the sections by size, putting the longest garments at one
end and the shortest at the other end. You can further sort your
clothes by colour. One suggestion is to do this by the colours of

the rainbow. Then order by sleeve length and seasonal weight.
If your item of clothing isn't in its spot, it's in the wash. Coat
hangers should face away from you because they're easier to
remove, and if the hangers are all facing in the same direction,
you can remove more than one item at a time. Store spare
hangers at the end of the rod so you don't waste time searching
for them.

DID YOU KNOW? To deter moths, silverfish, dust mites and other
insects, place 1 camphor ball, 4 cloves, a head of lavender, a
couple of drops of eucalyptus oil and 2 bay leaves in a small
muslin bag, tie it, then hang it on the rod in your wardrobe. It
will also make your clothes smell fresh and lovely!

DRAWER LINERS

There is a perception that drawer liners are very last century, but I
think they're a great protection for clothes. Not only do they deter
silverfish and mould, they also keep your clothes smelling fresh.
Modern drawers generally aren't finished well and clothes can
catch on splinters or rough plastic lugs. Use liners and you'll cut
back on time spent mending! All you have to do is place them on
the bottom of each drawer in your chest of drawers. You can
either buy them or make your own.

How to make drawer liners

Buy some acid-free paper from an art supplies shop. Acid-free
paper will prevent yellowing in clothes. Fill a spray bottle with
warm water, add 1 tea bag and leave for 3 minutes. Remove
the tea bag and add a couple of drops of oil of cloves and
some of your favourite perfume, then spray over the paper.

This mixture is particularly good for winter woollens and the tannins from the tea help prevent dust mites. Allow the paper to dry, then cut it to size and place it in your drawers. Replace them once a year. You could even match your draw liners to your bedroom's decoration scheme, as my mother does!

ALLERGY AGONY: Jodi's call to Shannon on radio

Q: INCIDENT: 'My husband is allergic to dust mites,' says Jodi. 'Is there any way of getting rid of them?'

SOLUTION: Dust mites hate tannins so the best way to get rid of them is with tea. Place 2 tea bags in a spray bottle of water and leave for 5 mintues. Remove the tea bags and then lightly spray the mixture over your mattress and pillows. Do this weekly. Another suggestion is to suck a damp tea bag into the vacuum cleaner before vacuuming. I always keep a damp tea bag nearby and sniff it when allergies hit. It's a life saver!

DID YOU KNOW? It doesn't matter how clean you are, you can get bed bugs. They've become more of a problem because fewer people like using cockroach bombs plus the formula in insecticide sprays has changed to an attractant. It's become such a problem that the tourism industry is holding summits on what to do about these tiny creatures that have taken up residence in hostel and hotel beds across the world! Bed bugs are about

3 mm long and look like flat leaves. The best way to get rid of them is with a cockroach bomb. If you don't like chemicals, wipe the bottom of furniture with tea tree oil or oil of pennyroyal. **Don't use oil of pennyroyal if anyone in the house is pregnant.** Wipe it along all the skirting boards and window frames. Wash all your bedding and dry it in the sun. The sun is a great antibacterial, anti-fungal and insecticide. You can also have a mattress commercially sanitised and debugged if needed. The procedure I've heard about uses a tea and UV formula. If you've been bitten by a bed bug, stop the itching by applying mint tea to the bite. To make mint tea, add 2 teaspoons of dried mint or 3 teaspoons of fresh mint to 240 ml of hot water. Allow the tea to steep for 2 minutes, then strain it. If desperate, you can apply mint sauce, which is made of vinegar, sugar and mint, directly to the itch. But don't use mint jelly because it's full of protein and will make the itchiness worse! You could even add mint to your bath water for relief. To stop the bites, rub lavender oil over your entire body before going to bed.

Kill dust mites by putting a tea bag into a spray bottle filled with cold water, let it sit for 3 minutes and then lightly spray it over the mattress. The tannins in tea kill dust mites.

HINT

Mosquitoes in the middle of the night
You're lying in bed, half asleep, when a high-pitched buzzing begins somewhere near your ear. The dreaded mozzie! You start whacking your face in the vain hope of killing it. But if the noise stops, it generally means one thing: you're being bitten. The best solution is lavender oil. Keep a bottle beside your bed. When you hear buzzing, put a drop on your pillowcase and

another drop on your hands, then rub it all over your body and
face. A couple of drops is enough for one person. You could
even put a couple of drops in a spray bottle of water and
spray it over you and the bed before going to sleep. Lavender
oil has the triple purpose of keeping mosquitoes away,
soothing the bite and assisting with sleep. I've even used a
novelty spray fan to help deal with the problem.

PILLOW AND MATTRESS PROTECTORS

Another way to save cleaning time in the bedroom is to use pillow
protectors. These quilt-like covers equalise the pressure of your
head on the pillow and help keep the pillow aerated. They allow
more air to flow so your head sweats less and produces less oil, so
you're less likely to get acne because everything stays cleaner.
They'll even keep you warmer in winter, acting like a thermos. The
same applies with mattress protectors. More air is able to flow, so
there's less sweat. A mattress is a difficult thing to wash or remove
stains from, which is another reason why a mattress protector is a
time saver. If you can't afford a mattress protector or don't like
them, use a pure woollen blanket that can be bought very
cheaply and already sanitised from charity shops.

HINT

This may seem excessive but it's a good habit to get into. Strip
your bed every day, let it air for at least 2 minutes, then remake
the bed with the same sheets. Air pillows once a week either
outside in the sun or over a chair near the window. UV is great at
killing bacteria. Fluff the pillows up before returning them to the
bed. Your bed will feel drier and fresher everyday, not just when
you change the sheets. If you can easily fold a pillow in half, it's
time for a new one!

If your mattress is damp, speed up the drying process with
a hairdryer.

If your child is a constant vomiter, keep a bucket or bowl in their
bedroom with fresh towels for instant mop ups. If you catch vomit
in a bucket and with a towel, it makes cleaning much easier.
You could also use a wastepaper bin with a solid bottom. Do
whatever you can to stop vomit getting into the mattress. Rinse
the soiled towel first then put it through the washing machine.

SHEETS

Sheets should be washed once a week. **Cotton** sheets can be washed
with washing powder or liquid in hot water. If they have blood or
other protein stains, remove the stain with cold water and soap
before you wash. **Polyester/cotton-blend** sheets can also be washed
with washing powder or liquid in hot water. If they have blood or
other protein stains, remove with cold water and soap before you
wash. **Flannelette** sheets can be washed with washing powder/liquid
in hot water. If they have blood or other protein stains, remove with
cold water and soap before you wash. **Egyptian cotton** sheets have a
larger thread count so the weave is stronger, finer and smoother.
Wash them with washing powder or liquid in hot water. If they have
blood or other protein stains, remove stains with cold water and soap
before you wash. **Linen** sheets should be washed with washing
powder or liquid in hot water. **Satin** sheets should be washed in cool
water. Hang the sheets over the clothesline so the satin sides rest
against each other. Remove the sheets from the line before they're
completely dry and partially fold them. That way you won't have to
iron them. Wash **silk** sheets with shampoo in blood-heat water and
add a little hair conditioner to blood-heat rinse water.

To make your sheets lovely and smooth, use rice-water starch. The next time you boil rice, drain and reserve the water (this obviously doesn't work if you cook rice by the absorption method!). Then mix 240 ml of the rice-water starch with 240 ml plain water. Add 120 ml of this mixture to the rinse cycle of the washing machine. Don't use rice-water starch on satin sheets because it will affect their texture and smoothness. Sleeping on a plastic bag would be more comfortable!

COMMON SPILLS ON SHEETS

Nail polish

Put a cotton wool ball behind the stain then soak another cotton wool ball in acetone (not nail polish remover) and rub it in a circular motion on the front of the stain. Use the dry cotton wool ball as backing. Work from the outside to the inside of the stain. Keep on doing this until all the colour is removed, replacing the cotton wool balls as you go. With some nail polish, this process will need to be repeated up to five times.

Coffee

For a new stain, use soap and cold water and rub the stain vigorously, then wash normally. For an old stain, apply glycerine and leave for 10–15 minutes, then put the sheets through the washing machine.

Chocolate

Because chocolate contains protein, you must use cold water. Dampen some soap in cold water, rub over the stain then soak the sheets in cold water. Wash the sheets in the washing machine on a warm or hot cycle. If the fabric is polyester satin, use dry cleaning fluid applied with a cotton wool ball against the stain and another cotton wool ball at the back of the stain. Rub in a circular motion working from the outside to the inside of the stain, then wash normally.

Blood

Dampen some soap in cold water and rub over the stain. Rub the stain against itself vigorously until it's removed. You may need to do this a few times. Put the sheets through the washing machine on the cold cycle. An alternative is to soak the stained item in **Vanish** If the stain has set, apply glycerine with a cotton wool ball to either side of the stain, rub in circles from the outside to the inside of the stain until it starts to shift at the edge then wash in **Vanish** and cold water.

Vomit

Rinse the sheet with water and put it through the washing machine. If the staining is particularly bad, soak in *Vanish* first then put through the washing machine.

DUVETS

Duvets can be made of goose feathers, wool or synthetics. Wash them twice a year or even more if you sweat a lot. You can tell it's time for a wash when the fibres are packed down and lumpy or the duvet is smelly. Some duvets can be put through the washing machine. Just check the manufacturer's instructions first. Others, regardless of the filling, can be washed in a bath or a large washing sink. If you don't have one, try to use a friend's.

As outlined in *Spotless*, this is my technique for washing a duvet. Fill the bath with warm water and half a cap of Woolite or shampoo for a double bed-sized duvet. Lay the duvet in the bath then get in yourself and stomp up and down on the duvet until you get rid of all the dirt and grime. Empty the bath, fill it again with clean blood-heat water, stomp over it again, then let the water out. For the final rinse, fill the bath again with clean blood-heat water and allow it to soak into the duvet.

After you've rinsed it, drain the water from the bath and tread on the duvet to squeeze out as much moisture as possible. Then take the duvet outside and put it on an old sheet. If you don't have a lawn, place it flat over the top of an airer. Leave it to dry for quite some time, then shake it and turn it. You need to do this about three times until it's almost dry. Then hang it on the airer using lots of pegs so you don't have the stress on any one spot. Unless you already have a stitched ridge, don't fold it over the line. Instead, peg it by the two outside edges on separate lines so the duvet forms a U-shape. This allows air to circulate. When it's almost completely dry, give it a whack with your hand or an old tennis racquet. This fluffs up the fibres or loosens the feathers and is great for stress relief. Put it inside a clean duvet cover to protect it against spills and grime.

If you can't be bothered washing your duvet, at least hang it on the clothesline in the sun to allow the UV rays to kill bacteria.

CHILDREN'S BEDROOMS

Help your children get into good cleaning habits. Keep a dirty clothes' basket in their room and show them how to use it. Place beds away from the wall so they can tuck the sheets in. Attach labels to drawers with pictures of what's inside to help them sort their clothes. Use plastic tubs to store toys. Create a specific area to do homework and creative pursuits. Have simple shelving units and lots of them. Keep a big wastepaper bin in the room.

DID YOU KNOW? If you're having trouble sleeping:
Have a glass of warm milk before you go to bed.
Wash your feet in cold water, dry them, then go to bed.
Put lavender and thyme under your pillow. Lavender rubbed across your forehead will ease a migraine.
Play soothing music very softly.
Add turkey to your diet.
Make sure you've got a good pillow. If it's very old and compacted, it will be full of dust mites and skin cells so get a new one.

DAILY CHECKLIST FOR THE BEDROOM

- air and make the bed
- put away clothes and shoes, place dirty clothes in laundry basket
- empty bin

The Bathroom

The bathroom is one of the easiest rooms in the house to look after because it's designed to be cleaned – and when you've finished, the room sparkles from floor to ceiling. I've developed a method for cleaning the bathroom that is super-speedy, but slightly unusual. So I've also included a more conventional speedclean if my technique is too radical for you.

As you know, I love to clean with bicarb and vinegar but you may prefer to use proprietary products. Whatever you use, make sure you rinse any product thoroughly. Never use steel wool on any surface in the bathroom or you'll create scratch marks.

If you think your cleaning is slow…

THE KISS ME QUICK LADIES' FACE RUB FROM *LEE'S PRICELESS RECIPES*, 1817

1 gallon of spirits, $\frac{1}{4}$ ounce essence of thyme, 2 ounces essence of orange flowers, $\frac{1}{2}$ ounce essence of neroli, 30 drops of attar of roses, 1 ounce of essence of jasmine, $\frac{1}{2}$ ounce of essence of balm mint, 4 ounces of petals of roses, 20 drops of lemon oil, $\frac{1}{2}$ ounce of colorous aromaticus (amber gris). Mix and strain, apply to the face on a daily basis.

It's apparently good for wandering husbands…

ASSEMBLE THE CLEAN KIT

Clutter bucket – to transport displaced items; **bicarb** – cleaning agent; **white vinegar** – cleaning agent; **Gumption** – cleaning agent; **water** – cleaning and rinsing; **methylated spirits** – to clean mirrors; **cloth** (such as an old T-shirt) – to wipe surfaces and absorb water; **old stockings** – to clean soap scum; **nylon broom** – to sweep floors and clear cobwebs; **dustpan and brush** – to clear accumulated dirt; **vacuum cleaner** – to vacuum floors; **mop** – to wipe over floors; **bucket** – to hold water or to hold cleaning items; **rubber gloves** – to protect hands and provide grip; **spray bottle** – to spray vinegar; **old toothbrush** – to access tight corners; **nylon scrubbing brush** – to aid cleaning; **denture cleaner** – to remove marks in the bath; **lavender oil** – cleaner and fragrance; **oil of cloves** – to deter mould; **glycerine** – to prime surfaces; **detergent** – cleaning agent; **old towel** – to absorb water; **paper towel** – to absorb water; **sponge or rags** – to use as cleaning cloths.

SUPER SPEEDCLEAN

Remove anything that doesn't belong in the bathroom with your clutter bucket. Then remove any loose items, such as towels, toilet paper, toothbrushes and bin, and store them outside the bathroom. Put all the plugs in the sink holes, including the bath, and cover the shower drain hole. Run the water from all the taps on hot until the room is really steamy. Watch that you don't create a flood of water – and make sure you don't put the extractor fan on! Then remove the plugs. In these times of water restrictions, you may want to save water by cleaning straight after you or someone else in the house has had a shower. Now, it's time to get active.

WARNING If you have marble, make sure you dilute 1 part white vinegar to 5 parts water and rinse thoroughly. If you have unsealed wood, clean with black tea and vinegar.

Cover your head with a scarf or shower cap, blokes included, put on rubber gloves and stand in the middle of the room with bicarb in your hand. Have the bicarb either in its box with small puncture holes in the top or in a large shaker. Imagine you are on a merry-go-round at a fun park and move in a circle lightly shaking bicarb around the bathroom, including the sink and toilet. Three tablespoons should be enough for the whole bathroom.

Now, have a spray bottle with white vinegar in it and grab a
sponge or broom. Squirt sections of the bicarb with the spray
bottle and, while it's fizzing, scrub with the sponge or broom. Use
an old toothbrush to access corners. Do this right around the
room, including the walls. I think the best way to access walls is
with a clean broom, which, if you think about it, is really just like
a large nylon brush! Once you've scrubbed every surface,
including the towel rail, rinse with water or you can use a spray
bottle filled with water. Just be very careful around electrical
fittings. For really stubborn stains on your sink, bath, toilet or any
tiled surface, use Gumption on a cloth.

If your grout is mouldy, wipe with bicarb and vinegar and
scrub with an old toothbrush. To inhibit mould, add a couple of
drops of oil of cloves to the mixture.

If you have unsealed wood, vinyl wallpaper or other surfaces
that shouldn't be left wet, dry them with either old cloth nappies
or old towels from the rag bag. Tie the towelling to your broom
head with elastic bands and wipe the walls.

TO CLEAN EXTRACTOR FANS

Remove the grill, rinse it under warm water, dry with a towel then
replace. **Never touch the fan or you could electrocute yourself!**

If you can, buy some old cloth nappies from charity shops or
garage sales. They're cheap, the towelling is 100 per cent
cotton and is of a very high quality.

TO CLEAN THE TOILET

1. Flush the toilet to wet the sides of the bowl.
2. Sprinkle bicarb over the inside of the bowl.
3. Wipe the top of the cistern with one sponge dipped in bicarb and another sponge dipped in white vinegar.
4. Wipe the top of the lid, under the lid, the top of the seat and under the seat using bicarb and white vinegar and the two-sponge technique (see page 111).
5. Splash white vinegar over the bicarb in the bowl, then use a toilet brush to scrub, including up and around the rim.
6. Wipe the top of the rim with a sponge that's been dipped in white vinegar.
7. Wash the sponge in hot water and wipe rim again.
8. Flush.
9. Rinse the sponge in white vinegar and wipe the outside of the toilet bowl right to the floor, including the plumbing at the back.
10. Congratulations, you're done!

HINTS FOR BLOKES: Speed your cleaning by using the toilet brush each time you use the toilet. If you scrub it straight away, there will be less cleaning to do later. Leave the toilet brush inside the toilet as you flush and it will clean the brush as well.

DID YOU KNOW? Lavender oil removes light water staining in the toilet. Add 1 drop of lavender oil every three days to create a cleaning film. If the stain is really bad, add $1/2$ capful of descaler to the cistern water.

I don't like using toilet mats and toilet seat covers because they harbour bacteria, smells and they create more cleaning. But if you do have them, make sure you wash them once a week.

Clean taps with an old stocking. I suggest wrapping the stocking around the back of the taps and moving them backwards and forwards in a sawing action. You could also use an old toothbrush to access any hard-to-reach areas. Make sure you clean around the edging of all the drains.

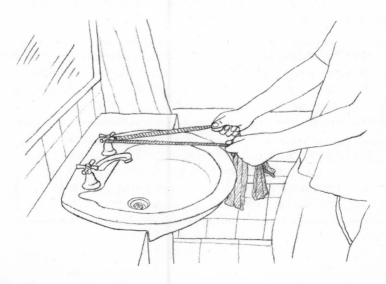

Mirrors should be cleaned with methylated spirits and a lint-free cloth, such as an old T-shirt. To prevent fogging, either scribble over the mirror with a bar of soap then polish it off with a cloth or wipe some spit over the mirror. I know it doesn't sound appealing, but it's how scuba divers keep their masks from fogging up!

DID YOU KNOW? Our sense of smell is very powerful, so if you use a fragrance normally associated with food in the bathroom, the smell centre in our brain registers it as wrong. It's best not to use fragrances associated with food, such as cinnamon, apricot or peach, in the bathroom. Lavender is my scent of choice.

Finish by drying surfaces, including the bath, with an old towel. You'll stop water marks and create a gleaming shine.

REGULAR SPEEDCLEAN

Clear the bathroom with a clutter bucket. Sprinkle bicarb over the bath, sink, shower and toilet. With white vinegar in a spray bottle, squirt the bicarb and scrub either with a sponge, scrubbing brush or a pair of old stockings rolled up into a ball. Stockings cut through soap scum really well. Clean behind taps by wrapping a stocking around the base of the taps and sawing backwards and forwards. Don't forget the areas around the drains. Clean the toilet as described on pages 96-97. Wipe the walls using the two-sponge technique (see page 111) or use one sponge dipped in bicarb and a spray bottle of vinegar. Clean a tiled floor by sprinkling over bicarb then spraying with white vinegar. As they're fizzing, rub over with a nylon brush or nylon broom. Rinse with water. Clean the mirror with methylated spirits and an old T-shirt.

Use a broom to access the ceiling and give it a good sweep. Then rinse the whole bathroom with water. After cleaning, towel dry all surfaces, including the bath. This prevents water marks and leaves a sparkling finish. To clean the inside of bathroom windows, use a squeegee and water. If the window is grimy, use 240 ml of white vinegar to a bucket of warm water.

HINT

Is it okay to use bleach?

Bleach is a cleaning agent and an antibacterial, but it's also quite corrosive and high in phosphates. Many people equate the smell of bleach to cleanliness, but if you can smell bleach it means the area hasn't been rinsed properly. Over time, it makes grout porous, strips the glaze off tiles, causes glass cancer on shower screens and breaks down the rubber sealant on shower screens. It even makes painted surfaces powdery. If you like cleaning with it, only use small diluted quantities and make sure you rinse thoroughly afterwards. I much prefer to use bicarb and white vinegar. Simply sprinkle on bicarb then sprinkle on vinegar and, when it's fizzing, scrub with a nylon brush or broom, then rinse.

HINT

If your bath has gone yellow

Bleach can often make modern bath surfaces turn yellow. Wipe the bath with glycerine on a cloth. Then wipe with dry cleaning fluid applied with a cloth. If that doesn't work, fill the bath with warm water and add 1 packet of denture tablets or powder. Leave overnight and drain the water.

HINT

If your bath has grey marks

It could mean bleach has taken off the porcelain coating and left an absorbent surface where dirt has lodged. To alleviate the problem, fill the bath with water and add 1 packet of denture cleaner. The denture cleaner can be in tablet or powder form. Leave overnight. Then wipe the surface with glycerine to seal it. If you use the bath often, you'll need to wipe the surface with glycerine every three months. The grey marks could also be created by contact with metallic objects such as steel wool or back scratchers made with stainless steel. Clean these marks by sprinkling on bicarb, adding white vinegar and scrubbing with a nylon brush or rub with a pencil eraser.

STRATEGIES TO MAKE CLEANING SPEEDIER

Ramp up your speedcleaning by tackling the task right after someone's had a steamy shower – the warm film of moisture is the perfect preparation base. Some people even clean while they're showering! One friend had great intentions of cleaning while he showered and even got to the point of leaving the cleaning bottle in the shower recess. It remained untouched until he noticed mosquitoes had started breeding in the moisture puddle under it! Keep a rolled up pair of pantyhose near the bath and have users wipe the bath down after having one. It'll help prevent those unattractive dirt rings and speed your cleaning. You could also keep a squeedgee in the shower recess and give the area a quick wipe after showering. If you have a shower curtain, leave it stretched open to dry so mould doesn't grow in the crevices.

HINT

> If there are several people in your home, wipe tea tree oil over the shower floor with a cloth after each shower to kill germs.

HINT

> **How to clean a streaky shower recess**
> If it's soap scum, mix 1 part methylated spirits, 1 part vinegar and 2 parts water and rub the mixture over the screen with a cloth. But if it's glass cancer, you're in trouble. Try rubbing it with goanna oil, if you can obtain some, or use sweet almond oil. Reapply sweet almond oil every time you clean. If that doesn't work, you may have to get a new shower screen!

The bathroom is an easy place for clutter to gather. I suggest having a stash of plastic tie bags so you can regularly remove clutter. If your cupboard space is under the sink, be careful what you store here because it can be a moisture trap. It's better to store items high and dry. Buy small storage units, preferably without doors, to organise all that bathroom paraphernalia, such as hair gel, cotton buds and dental floss.

ORGANISING THE VANITY UNIT
Allocate one shelf for each member of the family. Determine a spot on the shelf for each thing you store here and make sure you return items to this spot. It means you won't waste time searching for what you need. No matter how you store tooth-brushes, they will always attract bacteria – rinse them before and after cleaning your teeth. Replace them when the bristles start to bend, because if they're not straight, they won't work properly. Store with the bristles facing upwards and try not to let them come into contact with other toothbrushes. If they become

contaminated, throw them out or add them to your clean kit. However you store them, make sure you clean the holder and allow it to dry before putting the toothbrushes back in.

DAILY: Razors should be cleaned after each use. If you have an electric razor, clean it with a brush and sewing machine oil it each time you use it. Disposable razors should be cleaned by running your fingers from the lubricating strip down the blade, not against the blade, or you'll cut your fingers! If you prefer, use a soft sponge to clean it. It's a good idea to replace them often because bacteria is attracted to them. If you cut yourself a lot when shaving, keep a styptic pencil in the vanity unit. This has an alum base and shrinks blood vessels.

HINT

HINT FOR BLOKES: If you get whiskers in the sink after shaving, scrunch an old pair of tights into the shape of a tennis ball and wipe them away. Keep the tights under the sink so you can wipe each time you shave. If you don't have access to old tights, be manly and buy some cheap ones at the supermarket.

HINT

If you keep make-up in a bathroom drawer, make sure the bottom of the drawer is covered with 1 cm thick foam rubber, which is available from shops specialising in rubber products. It will provide a soft landing if you drop something. Store make-up in small plastic containers – old takeaway ones will do. Lift out the whole container when you use anything because you're less likely to drop it.

Thick foam rubber on the bottom of a drawer is also great protection for men's shaving gear.

If you drop foundation make-up on the floor
Blot with a paper towel. Then mix $1/2$ teaspoon of glycerine and $1/2$ teaspoon of detergent and apply to the stain. Massage the mixture into the stain with your fingertips, remove with a paper towel, then a damp cloth. Foundation has a fine grade oil and sticks to everything.

SHOWER HEADS

To keep your cleaning at top speed, watch out for hard-water fur or limescale in your shower head. That's when little black prickly things form in the nozzle. Unless you have brass fittings, get rid of them with descaler. Mix according to the directions on the packet in a bucket or ice-cream container and immerse the shower head in the solution. Leave for a few minutes until the solution is absorbed. Then turn on the shower and watch the black prickles fall down the drain. For any strays, use a needle to unblock the holes. Keep brass shower heads clean with equal parts white vinegar and lemon juice applied with an old toothbrush. Brass shower heads are generally big enough to scrub the hard-water fur out.

If you have a separate bath and shower, I suggest having two of everything – from soap to shampoo – so you're not constantly reaching from one area to another, especially when wet! And on the topic of soap, I think each family member should have their own bar of soap in the shower.

If there are drip marks in the bath or sink
Use a little descaler applied with a cotton wool ball, cotton bud or nylon brush.

DID YOU KNOW? Soap for washing your hands should have a slightly higher acidic base to help kill bacteria and cut through grease. I use lemon myrtle soap.

HINT

If you have problems with mould in the bathroom, try to allow as much ventilation as possible. To inhibit mould, add a couple of drops of oil of cloves to your rinse water.

TOWELS

I prefer to store towels away from the bathroom because they can get a musty smell from the steam. But if you do store them here, make sure they are kept under a shelf so moisture doesn't drop onto them – and don't roll them up because you will create a mould centre. After using them, towels must be allowed to dry on a towel rack or they'll smell and make you smell as well! Try to get as much air as possible through the towel, so hang it unfolded. If you don't have the space, fold it in two, reversing the fold each day. You can tell which side you've folded by the seam. If you don't have a towel rack, hang the towel on the clothesline. Keep a hand towel near the sink so your bath towel isn't used to dry hands.

Wash towels once a week. Keep them soft by adding bicarb to the wash water and vinegar to the rinse. Use warm water when washing dark towels to retain the colour.

Clean towel rails, including heated ones, with a cloth that's been wrung out in water.

The best bathroom mats use a high density towelling that absorbs water and stays stiff so you won't slip. Wash them once a week in the washing machine.

Always have a bin near the toilet. I also provide waxed brown paper bags that are waterproof for up to 6 months. They're ecological and make guests feel more comfortable. Having a bin near the toilet means there's no excuse for people leaving empty toilet rolls lying around near the toilet!

UNWANTED BLACK LINE: John's call to Shannon on radio

Q: INCIDENT: 'I've got a nasty black mark on the water line of my toilet,' says John. 'I just can't shift it. What should I do?'

SOLUTION: Place a capful of descaler into the cistern of the toilet. Leave it for 10 minutes then flush. Then leave it again for another 10 minutes. Then turn the tap off at the cistern and drain the water from the bowl with a small plastic cup. Then wipe the mark with bicarb and vinegar and scrub with a brush. Turn water back on then flush.

TOILET ROLLS

In days gone by, Barbie-like dolls called 'dress-a-dolls' became a popular toilet-roll storage solution. Dolly's legs would go through the centre of the roll and a colourful crocheted nylon dress would cover the toilet paper. Dolly was generally plonked on top of the cistern, her outfit often matching the toilet seat cover and mat. They were much loved by grandmothers, but if they only knew how much bacteria lived in the skirts, they'd be horrified! These days, many people keep spare toilet rolls on the cistern but I think you should avoid this because it's too easy for the roll to fall into the toilet. I store toilet rolls on a giant wooden spike with a thick base so water doesn't get onto the bottom of the toilet paper and make it frilly. Pile them as high as you like or use several spikes. I use unscented toilet rolls because many people are sensitive to the chemicals. If you like having a scent, you can create your own. Simply spray a small amount of lavender oil onto the cardboard inside the toilet roll. Cardboard absorbs the lavender smell and continually recirculates it.

DIRTY-LOOKING BATH: Joanne's call to Shannon on radio

Q: INCIDENT: 'We live in the Australian bush,' says Joanne. 'And use dam water which has really stained the bath. Is there any way of repairing it?'

SOLUTION: Use a descaler and follow the instructions on the packet with one variation. Dilute the mixture to half the recommended strength. Then wipe it over the surface of the bath with a cloth. Then rinse with water.

HINT

Create your own air freshener by filling a spray bottle with water, add 2 drops of detergent and 5 drops of lavender oil. Leave it near the toilet. You can also use tea tree oil or any of the floral essential oils.

TOYS

Anyone with young children will
have an array of toys in the bath.
To help with cleaning, and to
avoid sitting or stepping on a
sharp piece of plastic, keep a toy
net in the bathroom. You can
easily make your own. Buy some
nylon netting, which comes in a
variety of colours, from a
hardware shop. Attach two large
stainless steel curtain rings to
either end, then pull the ends
together and thread with a cord.
Hang the toy net on a hook in
the bathroom where it can drain.
You could also reuse orange
netting bags from the fruit
market if there's only a small
number of toys – and if orange goes with your bathroom.

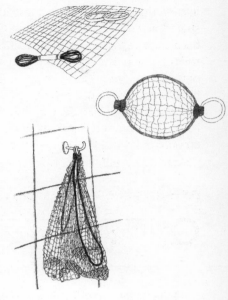

HINT

If your bath or sink plugs are difficult to remove, attach a
curtain ring, a length of nylon cord or a ball chain to the top.
Ball chains are available from hardware shops.

DAILY CHECKLIST FOR THE BATHROOM

- · **wipe the sink and bath with rolled-up pantyhose**
- · **use the toilet brush to clean the loo**
- · **check there's toilet paper**
- · **empty bin**

The Kitchen

I know it sounds obvious, but because food is stored and prepared in the kitchen, this is the most important room in the house to keep clean. Be vigilant about cleaning surfaces and floors. Any scrap of food, whether you can see it or not, will attract bugs. Be guided by your nose because it's great at sniffing out any missed scraps – especially those dropped by children. This is the most intensive room for daily and speedcleaning.

> If you think your cleaning is slow...
>
> ### How to freshen marble from *Lee's Priceless Recipes*, 1817
>
> Mix 1 bullock's gall with 4 ounces of soap lees and 2 ounces of turpentine. Add sufficient pipe clay to make it into a paste. Apply to the marble and leave for 24 hours, then rub it off. If it's not clean, repeat until it is. It could take several days.

ASSEMBLE THE CLEAN KIT

Clutter bucket – to transport displaced items; **bicarb** – cleaning agent and absorbent; **vinegar** – cleaning agent; **detergent** – cleaning agent; **glycerine** – stain softener; **vanilla essence** – fragrance and antiseptic; **table salt** – to deter cockroaches; **spray bottle** – to hold either vinegar or water; **vacuum cleaner** – to vacuum floors; **damp cloth** – to wipe over surfaces; **methylated spirits** – to clean glass; **lavender oil** – fragrance; **old T-shirt** – to use as cleaning rag; **elastic band** – to secure old T-shirt to broom head; **broom** – to clean floors and walls; **sponge** – to wipe over surfaces; **old stockings** – to wipe over surfaces and behind taps; **old toothbrush** – to access tight corners; **paper towel** – to wipe over surfaces; **rags** – to use as cleaning cloths; **refuse sacks** – to hold rubbish; **storage box** – to hold items; **washing-up brush** – for washing up.

SPEEDCLEAN

The best time to clean the kitchen is before doing the weekly shop because there's less food to work around. Begin the speed-clean by putting anything that doesn't belong in the kitchen into your clutter bucket. Once you've done this, leave the clutter bucket outside the kitchen. Items can be returned to their proper spots later on.

HINT

What is the two-sponge technique?
The two-sponge technique is used to clean vertical surfaces. Wring one sponge out in water then dip it in a tray of bicarb. Wring another sponge in vinegar. Place the bicarb sponge on the surface to be cleaned, then put the vinegar sponge over the back of it and use your hand to push the two sponges together. This allows the vinegar to mix with the bicarb and create the all-important cleaning fizz.

FRIDGE

In *Spotless*, I recommend cleaning the fridge once a month, but each week, you should remove items from the fridge and wipe over the shelves and crispers using either the two-sponge technique or a sponge wrung out in white vinegar with bicarb added. To rinse clean, wipe with a cloth that's been wrung out with water.

For the monthly clean of the fridge, have one storage box and one bin bag with you. Put all the food that's gone off in the bin bag and the other food in the storage box so that you have easy access to the fridge. It's much easier to wipe over a clear shelf than crash and move your jars around as you clean! Using the two-sponge technique (see page 111), wipe all the shelves, compartments and sides of the fridge. Leave the door open for 2 minutes so the vinegar can vaporise or it will leave the fridge smelling a bit pickled. Then, if there's any residue, wipe with a cloth wrung out in water. If you like a fragrance, I suggest using vanilla essence. Vanilla has a strong alcohol base, is an antiseptic and the smell won't taint food. It also helps absorb odours, which is why I like to keep a two-sided container in the fridge – one side with bicarb in it, the other with vanilla essence. Return the items from the storage box to the fridge.

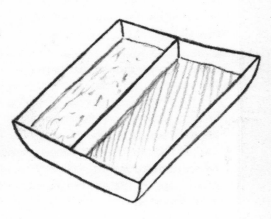

HINT

Line the base of the crispers in your fridge with a 5-mm thick piece of foam rubber. This stops food getting caught in the ridges and slows the rotting process because air circulates around the food. Your lettuce won't turn to slime! Foam rubber is available from specialist kitchen shops and department stores. Wash it with detergent and water each time you clean the fridge and dry it on the clothesline.

Many freezers are auto-defrost. Those that aren't need to be defrosted regularly because excess ice transfers flavours from one food source to another. If your ice-cream has been tasting a bit fishy lately, it means there's too much ice in the freezer! Even auto-defrost freezers have to be cleaned occasionally. Defrost when ice is greater than 5 mm thick. To do this, remove everything from the fridge and freezer, throw out anything past its use-by date (as marked when the item was first put in the freezer), store other items in an ice-filled cool bag, turn the fridge off and allow the ice to melt. Clean thoroughly before turning the fridge back on and returning the items. To keep ice at bay, dip a cloth in a solution of 1 tablespoon of white sugar to 240 ml of just-warm water, then wipe the cloth around the freezer. Sugar slows down the production of ice.

Never put a bowl of hot water into a freezer. You could crack the coils and the steam produces more ice crystals. Instead, sprinkle some white sugar over the ice and it will melt more quickly. Sugar doesn't freeze. **Never use a hairdryer or heater inside the freezer** because it could crack the coils and is very dangerous. **Never use a sharp knife** or you could pierce the compartment and release the gas, which is also dangerous. Instead, remove the ice with a rubber spatula or with gloved hands.

OVEN

Even if you haven't used the oven you should clean it. I know this sounds odd, but because it's a dark space, insects like to get inside. Remove the oven racks and supports. Then clean the oven with bicarb and vinegar using the two-sponge technique (see page 111). Clean the oven glass in the same way. For stubborn stains, scrub with a small nylon washing-up brush after applying the two sponges, then rinse with water. If you'd like to see how well you're cleaning the top of the oven without craning your neck, place a small mirror on the bottom of the oven. Clean the racks and supports with bicarb and vinegar using the two-sponge technique. For stubborn build-up, add bicarb directly to the nylon washing-up brush and scrub along the rack. If the build-up on the racks is really bad, use a plastic scourer. **Never use a scourer inside the oven or you'll scratch it**. Let the racks stand before rinsing in water. Allow racks to dry then replace. Clean the stovetop by sprinkling over bicarb then spraying with vinegar, wipe with a cloth, then rinse with a cloth wrung out in water. Gas rings should be removed and cleaned in water and a little detergent. Make sure all the rings are clear before putting them back. With electric stove tops, remove the elements and rings, then clean with bicarb and vinegar. Make sure you don't allow the electric ports to get damp.

Clean the outside of the fridge, microwave, dishwasher and appliances with a sponge dampened with a little white vinegar. If you have grimy surfaces, add a little bicarb to the vinegar cloth, but vinegar should be enough to do the job. If there's staining on plastic surfaces, wipe with glycerine first.

Wipe the front of cupboard doors, the splashback and wipe the tops of canisters. If you have glass in your cupboard doors, clean with methylated spirits and a lint-free cloth. Don't forget to wipe the range hood and to check the filter, particularly if you're using it a lot. If it's looking greasy, wash the filter according to the manufacturer's instructions.

MICROWAVE

Check the inside of the microwave. Ideally, you should clean the inside of the microwave as soon as any mess is made, but if you haven't, do it now. If old food is caked on, mix 120 ml white vinegar, 240 ml of water and 1 tablespoon of bicarb in a large microwave-safe bowl. Put the bowl in the microwave without a lid and cook on high. The amount of time you leave it cooking will depend on the strength of your microwave. Allow the mixture to boil, but not boil over, for around 1 minute. While it's warm and steamy, wipe the interior with a cloth.

DID YOU KNOW? To remove rust marks on plastic, use a paste of glycerine and talcum powder and polish it off.

When cooking on a gas stovetop, save energy by having the flame only touch the bottom of the pot, not curling around it. Those flames curling around the pot are simply warming the kitchen, not the pot.

DISHWASHER

Clean inside the dishwasher once a week with bicarb and vinegar using the two-sponge technique (see page 111). To stop the plumbing from becoming corroded, run the dishwasher empty once a week with bicarb in the soap compartment and white vinegar in the rinse aid compartment. If the dishwasher is really stinky, wipe the rubbers and interiors with vanilla essence. This removes the smell and acts as an antibacterial – if the rubbers become perished, they harbour bacteria. To help prevent perishing, rub the surfaces with dry table salt and then vanilla essence. Remove and clean the filter at the bottom of the dishwasher.

If you have cockroaches, make sure they don't get inside the front of the dishwasher and into the liquid crystal display because it can short the dishwasher. To stop them getting in, wipe around the seals of the dishwasher with a cloth wrung out in table salt and water. Keep the kitchen free of crumbs and other cockroach food supplies. Alternatively, you can spray the surrounds, but not the interior, of the dishwasher with insecticide.

HINT

How to stack and unstack the dishwasher speedily
Always rinse off any food before putting items in the dishwasher. To speed your stacking, put like items, such as plates, together. Put matching cutlery in the same compartment, so all knives, for example, sit together. It makes unstacking quicker. Heat-sensitive items, such as plastics, should sit at the top, saucepans should sit at an angle towards the bottom centre of the dishwasher – and don't overpack because china and glass can break if they bang together. If tightly packed it doesn't clean properly. Never put electrical parts in. Always use a good-quality soap and rinse agent. **Never put fine china, good silver, crystal, items with gold edging or silver-plated, brass and gold-plated cutlery in the dishwasher.**

After you've stacked the dishwasher, check that the propeller in the middle of the machine can spin freely so that water spreads throughout the interior. Also check that the spray jets are clear and avoid the embarrassment that a friend of mine had when she received a lecture from a repairman for allowing her jets to clog. Have the top shelf raised or lowered to suit the size of your plates. This will make using it speedier.

HINT

HINTS FOR BLOKES: If you're going to wash the rocker cover from the car in the dishwasher, make sure you wash inside the dishwasher immediately after you've finished. Run it empty with bicarb in the detergent compartment and vinegar in the rinse compartment or there will be grease on the next load of dishes. Your missus won't be happy and your dinner will taste funny.

 DID YOU KNOW? To remove egg stains from a pan, place half an egg shell with a strip of aluminium foil and 240 ml of vinegar into the stained pan. Leave for half an hour and wipe off with a nylon washing-up brush or sponge.

HINT
If there's a smell in the sink drain, put 50 g of bicarb down the drain, followed immediately by 120 ml of vinegar. Leave for half an hour. If it's still smelly, do it again. If you have copper or brass pipes, it will smell worse for about half an hour before it gets better. Once rinsed through with water, however, the smell will dissipate.

CUPBOARDS AND DRAWERS

 Quickly wipe inside cupboards every couple of weeks. Clean surfaces with a cloth that's been wrung out in a little detergent and water.

 Wipe along the pantry shelves, but don't worry about extensive cleaning until the spring clean. The easiest way to clean inside your kitchen drawers is to vacuum them every couple of weeks, then wipe with a cloth wrung out in water. If you haven't cleaned them in a while, use bicarb and vinegar, then wipe with a cloth that has been soaked in hot water. If you have unsealed wooden kitchen drawers, clean with a cloth that's

been tightly wrung out in hot water then dry the area before
returning the utensils. These drawers should be sealed with contact
paper or a liner of some form because raw timber attracts insects
and isn't hygienic for cutlery.

DID YOU KNOW? To ripen any soft fruits, just put them in a
brown paper bag with a banana and place in a cupboard.
Bananas give off ripening chemicals called ethylene. Never
keep bananas in the fridge or they'll go black.

If you have toddlers, protect
the contents of cupboards
by fixing an elastic band
over the handles so they
can't open the doors.

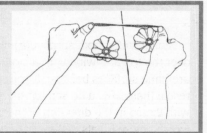

CHAIRS AND STOOLS

If you have chairs or stools in the kitchen, wipe them with a cloth
that's been wrung out in water because they are great dust
collectors. And don't forget to clean the legs as well.

DAILY: TABLES AND WORKTOPS

No matter how busy or tired you are, you must wipe tables and
worktops before going to bed. This is not an optional extra. If you
don't, your food preparation zone will become a feast's paradise for
nasties such as cockroaches. If you're wavering, just picture yourself
coming to the kitchen in the middle of the night to see something
scary scurrying across the worktop. It's the last thing you need.

WOOD

If wood is unsealed, clean with detergent and water and allow to dry. Wipe it with a good-quality furniture oil. For surfaces that come into contact with food, use a small quantity of warm olive oil. Some olive oils contain vegetable sediment, which can attract fruit fly, so make sure you spread it thinly and wipe off all the excess. Use olive oil only on wooden surfaces in the kitchen. Olive oil is safe to use around food but because it attracts fruit fly, it's not good to use outside the kitchen. Bicarb and vinegar will remove any stains, but remember to reapply the olive oil. If you prefer, keep the wood moist and splinter-free by rubbing it with the peel of a lemon.

For sealed wood, sprinkle some bicarb, then spray vinegar over the top and wipe with a cloth. Be very careful with polyurethane surfaces because if you scratch them, you'll have to reseal them. If you do scratch the surface of polyurethane, wipe it with Brasso in the direction of the grain. The mark will become worse before it gets better. Brasso works because it partially melts the polyurethane. If the scratch has penetrated through to the wood, you'll have to reseal the area which is a big job. If this is the case, seek the advice of a professional.

LAMINATE

The best way to keep laminate clean is to sprinkle over bicarb then spray with white vinegar and wipe with a sponge. If you get heavy staining with tea or scorch marks, put glycerine on the stain for about 5 minutes, then use bicarb soda and vinegar.

CORIAN

Clean by sprinkling bicarb then spraying white vinegar and wiping with a sponge. Use detergent and water for a polyurethane finish.

MARBLE

Special care should be taken with marble because the surface is porous. Clean with bicarb and 1 part white vinegar to 5 parts water. Never put full-strength vinegar on marble because it could react with the lime and eat into the marble. Always rinse thoroughly afterwards with a cloth that's been wrung out in water. If the surface isn't sealed with polyurethane or another sealant, use a good-quality liquid wax for marble flooring to make it less porous and less likely to absorb stains. The way to tell if marble is covered in polyurethane is to put your eye level with the marble surface and shine a light along the top. If the light shines in one uninterrupted beam, it's sealed with polyurethane. If the beam of light has lines and dots, it's unsealed.

GRANITE

Clean with bicarb and white vinegar. If it has a polyurethane finish, keep the surface clean because heat, abrasives, moisture and chemicals can cause it to bubble.

STAINLESS STEEL

The best way to clean stainless steel is with bicarb and vinegar, and then rinse off.

HINTS FOR KIDS: Children love things that fizz. Have them help you clean the worktops by sprinkling over some bicarb, then adding vinegar. They'll love the reaction the two make when they come into contact – the fizzing also tickles their fingers!

Make sure you wipe the whole work surface and don't forget the area underneath the toaster and kettle. These appliances may hide crumbs to your eyes, but cockroaches will sniff them out a street away.

DID YOU KNOW? To remove plastic bread wrapping that has melted onto the toaster, turn the toaster off, allow it to cool and clean with bicarb and vinegar applied with an old rolled-up stocking. If it's a large burn, use coarse rock salt applied with a damp toothbrush.

If you spill hot fat on a worktop, mop it up with a paper towel quickly. Hot fat can burn straight through laminate and can also dissolve glues, so speed is important. After clearing as much fat as possible, wipe the area with bicarb and white vinegar on a sponge.

Organise takeaway menus in a folder that has several transparent plastic sheets. Put one menu in each plastic sheet.

If you keep recipe books in the kitchen, wipe them each week and spray them with insecticide spray as they attract insects.

Sweep or vacuum the floors in preparation for mopping. I like to mop floors with a dampened old T-shirt wrapped around a broom head and secured by elastic bands – brooms are much better than mops at getting into corners. The temperature of your mopping water will vary according to the surface. Use cold water on cork, wood, old lino or any absorbent surface. Other surfaces can withstand hot water, which helps break down fats. Add 240 ml of vinegar to the water to make the surface non-slip.

Walls, skirting boards, cornices and the ceiling should be dusted regularly. If they're very dirty, dampen an old T-shirt in white vinegar and water, then wrap the T-shirt around a broom head, fix it with elastic bands and wipe it over the walls. Pay particular attention to the area above the stove.

TAPS AND SINKS

Clean the taps on sinks, including the base, with an old stocking or toothbrush. Use the stocking in a see-saw action around the taps. Clean the sink and buff it. Gumption on a sponge is good for this.

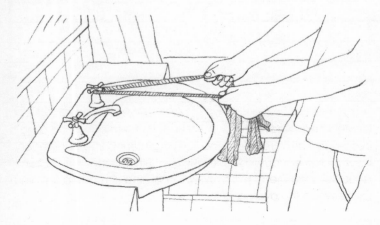

WINDOWS AND DOORS

Clean kitchen windows with methylated spirits and a lint-free cloth. If the windows are steamed up a lot, wipe them with white vinegar and a lint-free cloth first. Dust the doors with an old T-shirt, paying particular attention to the area near the door handle where hand marks often land!

STRATEGIES TO MAKE CLEANING SPEEDIER

 The best way to speedclean is to deal with spills and stains immediately. If you don't, the stains set and are harder to remove.

There are many ways to make your kitchen more efficient and manageable. You may be familiar with the idea of organising the kitchen in a triangle with the sink, fridge and oven forming each corner of the triangle. The chopping board should be located between the sink and the oven. Utensils should be kept between the chopping board and the oven.

 HINT

Have a tea towel under your chopping board to collect crumbs. Shake the contents straight into the bin.

 The direction you wash up, either left to right or right to left, will determine where plates and cutlery go. The aim is to have the smallest distance between the washing up rack and the cupboard shelves. The pantry should be as far away from the sink and stove as possible because of heat and damp. It's best located near the fridge so you can gather items from this area in one go. I don't recommend keeping utensils in a canister on the worktop because bugs can get in. Either hang utensils from a rack or store them in a drawer. Keep cling film and aluminium foil between the oven and the fridge.

HINT

Never operate an electric kettle underneath a cupboard because it will steam the bottom of the cupboard.

HINT

HINTS FOR BLOKES: Most men like to clean from one side of the kitchen to another, rather than doing one chore at a time. If this is the case for you, start cleaning from the sink and work around. When you're washing pots and pans, remember to wash the greasiest ones last so you don't transfer all that grease to the rest of the washing up.

Determine the airflow in the kitchen and the likely movement of grease and dust by turning on all your appliances, such as the oven, oven hood and dishwasher. Open the window as well, then light a candle and move around the kitchen making a note of how the flame bends in various spots. You'll be able to map how air moves in the kitchen and where grease and dirt are likely to land.

Work out where the congestion spots are and put some extra effort into cleaning these areas. Don't forget that heat from the dishwasher, oven, kettle and sink will rise.

HINT

If you boil new wooden utensils for 10 minutes in a saucepan with enough cider vinegar to cover them, it seals the wood and protects against smells and splintering. This is particularly good for wooden spoons used for making curries. To remove a curry stain, soak the wooden spoon in glycerine for a couple of days, then wash.

Sweeten the smell of a room where curry has been cooked, by slicing a lemon, placing it on a saucer and pressing down on the lemon to release its juices. It gives the room a fresh rather than a stale smell.

HINT

If you drop an egg on the floor, don't use a sponge to clean it up or you'll spread the mess. If you have a pair of squeegees (see page 14), push them together and lift the egg into a bowl. If you don't have squeegees, get two pieces of thick cardboard, place them either side of the egg spill, and move them towards each other, collecting the egg as you go. Place the egg in a bowl then throw it in the bin. When most of the egg has been removed, use a paper towel dampened with detergent to eradicate all traces of the mess. Always use cold water as cooked egg is harder to remove.

DETERGENT

Detergent acts as an emulsifier for fats and oils, which means it allows grease to mix with water and helps lift it off surfaces. Oils and fats are what make most types of dirt stick to other objects. When you break them down, you make it easier to clean off the dirt. Detergents are not all antibacterial, though many people assume they are. The other mistake people make is using too much detergent when washing up – **more is not better**. If you use too much, you'll have to rinse items after washing up because it will leave a soap residue – and bacteria can thrive in soap residue! You simply need to balance the amount of detergent with the amount of grease you're cleaning. With a good-quality liquid, 1 teaspoon of detergent per sink of hot water should be plenty. You can tell by the amount of bubbles in the water. You need only 2 cm of foam on the top of the water for a standard sink of dishes. When the bubbles disappear, it's time for some fresh water and detergent. Once all the washing up has been done and the dish rack is stacked, tip a jug of warm water over the clean dishes to rinse away any detergent. Allow the water to drain, leaving the dishes clean and shiny. Then, if you must, dry them with a clean tea towel.

DAILY: After washing up, clean your rubber gloves by taking them off, turning them inside out and putting them back on your hands inside out. Wash your gloved hands with soap, remove the gloves and stand them on the edge of the sink to dry inside out. You could also hang them over two wooden spoons formed in an X-shape.

HINT

If the kitchen sink has overflowed, turn off the water, mop the worktops with a sponge or mountains of paper towel, wipe the tops and fronts of cupboard doors and wipe the shelves, then mop the floor. Because moisture encourages cockroaches and mould, leave the cupboard doors open for at least 24 hours. If it's still damp, leave the doors open until the interior is completely dry. To speed the cleaning, stand a heater in front of the cupboards but monitor it closely. When dry, wipe any surfaces again with a damp cloth impregnated with a couple of drops of oil of cloves to inhibit mould growth. Mould spores grow very easily.

DAILY: TEA TOWELS

I suggest changing tea towels every two days but if you use the tea towel for anything other than drying, such as an oven mitt or for catching crumbs and wiping hands, be on the safe side and put it in the wash every day. After using them, hang tea towels out to dry or bacteria will breed in them. To clean tea towels, wash them in the washing machine or, if they're really soiled, first soak them in Vanish before putting them through the washing machine.

HINT

If you're making cakes, speed your cleaning by standing the mixing bowl on a dampened tea towel. The tea towel collects any dropped ingredients, such as flour. Its contents can then be shaken into the bin.

KITCHEN CLOTHS

There is an increasing range of kitchen cloths and sponges available these days. While the newer ones are much better at picking up dirt, they're also more likely to hold bacteria because of the greater surface area. Those hairy bits simply offer more spots for bacteria to live in. My preference is to recycle rags from the rag bag. There's no need to buy expensive cleaning cloths when an old T-shirt does the job really well. Either rip up the old T-shirt or cut it with scissors to the size you need. An important rule with kitchen cloths is not to contaminate your food preparation area. I suggest using different coloured sponges or cloths according to where they're used. I use green sponges for the worktops and pink sponges for the floor. I use yellow and blue sponges or cloths in the bathroom. Place sponges in a small bowl of vinegar, leave overnight then rinse in hot water.

Replace the nylon washing-up brush when the bristles are bent out of shape, but don't throw away the worn ones. Keep them for other uses, such as to clean outside under ledges and around pot plants in the garden and for scrubbing spot stains on the kitchen floor.

GLASSES, PLATES AND DISHES

Should you store glasses facing up or down?

This is a guaranteed conversation starter and a bit like the debate over which way the toilet paper should hang. This is what I do and why I do it. Glasses stored on shelves above eye level should face upwards to remind you to rinse them out before using them. This is because you can't see if the shelves are dusty. Glasses stored on shelves below eye level should face downwards. This is because you can see if the cupboard shelf is dirty and if the glass needs to be rinsed before using it.

DID YOU KNOW? If you drop a glass on the ground, make sure you've collected all the shards by lying a lit torch on the floor so the beam goes across the floor. Any remaining shards will sparkle in the light. Make sure you wear shoes and gloves when clearing glass.

In terms of where plates and dishes should be stored, I apply the principle that anything you eat off should be stored above waist height because of bugs. Anything kept below waist level should be washed before being used. Make sure pots and pans are completely dry before putting them away to prevent mould and corrosion.

Don't store china and metal on top of one another because the metal will leave a 'tile mark', which is like a pencil mark. To remove, use a soft pencil eraser.

THE THIRD-DRAWER SYNDROME

I don't know why, but everyone has the 'third-drawer syndrome'. This is the drawer that holds all the miscellaneous items, such as spare batteries, sticky tape, string and light bulbs. It's the drawer that tends to be a mess and takes ages to find anything in. Only kitchen paraphernalia, such as twine, thermometers and skewers should be kept in this drawer and in designated spots. You're not allowed just to open the drawer, throw in the item and apply the 'out of sight, out of mind' approach. Other items, especially batteries, should be kept elsewhere, such as the office, because moisture in the kitchen can damage them.

MR DISASTER: Ken's call to Shannon on radio

Q: INCIDENT: 'We call our 8-year-old son, "Mr Disaster",' confides Ken. 'Recently, he decided to clean our laminex worktop with a scourer and has managed to take all the gloss off. The colour is fine, it's just affected the sheen which is now a bit hazy.'

SOLUTION: There's a spray called Ceramicoat. It's very fast drying so do a test patch first so you become familiar with how it works. Prepare the surface first by sprinkling some bicarb over the area, then sprinkle some vinegar and rub with a nylon brush. Then rinse with a cloth that's been wrung out in water. Make sure the surface is completely dry, then apply the ceramicoat in thin, even layers. Ceramicoat is available at ceramics shops.

HINT

Store kitchen twine in a plastic zip-lock bag and create a small hole in the plastic to thread the twine through. It means the twine is protected and hygienic enough to use on roasts and other cooking.

PANTRY

You will be speedier in the kitchen if your pantry is well organised. Keep like items together, such as tins, so you don't waste time searching for them. Keep grain foods separately because bugs are attracted to them. As soon as you open any packet, the contents should go into a container rather than being left out to attract moths, cockroaches, weevils and other nasties. If you do get moths, use bay leaves or bay oil. Two bay leaves per shelf should do the job. Add a couple of drops of bay oil to a cloth and wipe over the shelves. If you have a serious bug problem, wipe the shelves once a month. If you don't have a serious bug problem, wipe the shelves once every three months. Oil of pennyroyal is another option **but not if anyone in the house is pregnant**. If you don't have containers or room for containers, fold over the top of a packet three times, then seal it with a bulldog clip or peg. Reorganise the pantry during the spring and autumn cleans.

CUPBOARD TOPS

Another way to save cleaning time in the kitchen is to put old newspaper on the tops of cupboards. Many kitchen cupboards now go right up to the ceiling, which removes this task, but if you have exposed cupboards, you'll be amazed at how much dust and grease gathers here. The reason it's an issue is that dust and grease travel around the kitchen. Replace the newspaper each month. It's much easier doing this than scrubbing later on. If you have layers of dust and grease, I've developed a really strong cleaner but it is very reactive and could eat into some finishes, such as gloss paints, wallpaper, printed pattern contact and unsealed wood, so don't use it on areas that can be seen.

Shannon's Toxic Cleaner

In a jar, mix 75 g of grated soap, 2 tablespoons of methylated spirits, 120 ml of vinegar and 2 tablespoons of bicarb. Seal the jar and shake it until all the ingredients are dissolved. Apply with a cloth. This can also be used on the top of enamel or copper oven hoods, on top of the fridge and in the garage to clean grease from tools. It's not really toxic, but can eat through certain surfaces.

If you've got some greasy build-up on your cupboards, you can soften it with steam from the kettle.

COMMON KITCHEN PESTS

COCKROACHES

The cockroach is high on most people's list of most-hated pests. And they are really difficult to get rid of. Here are a couple of strategies. The first is a chemical option using a proprietary cockroach spray. Several are available and I recommend one with an egg-killing function. Make sure you follow the instructions on the insecticide can carefully and avoid spraying directly onto food preparation areas. Every night, just before going to bed, spray around the skirting boards of the kitchen. Also spray around the fridge, which generally provides a warm home for cockroaches. This will reduce the cockroach supply. You'll need to be more vigilant in the summer months, but continue spraying in winter. Cockroaches are still around but don't breed as quickly. The non-chemical option uses salt. I use swimming pool salt because it's much cheaper, but table salt works just as well. Using a salt shaker, scatter salt along the edge of the skirting board in the kitchen, including under the fridge. Salt is absorbed through the underside carapace of the cockroach which dehydrates and kills them. One reason they're so hard to kill is that before they die, they drop their egg case, which, in German cockroaches, contains about 40 eggs that hatch in 28–30 days. If the egg case falls on the salt, the nymphs that hatch out dehydrate and die. It is also a good idea to rinse around drains with a salt solution and use flyscreen netting underneath floor wastes and drain holes. Cockroaches don't like salt and the netting stops larger ones from getting inside. The netting keeps spiders out as well. Cockroaches love moist, fatty, meaty, sweet, dark environments with lots of organic material. They stay away from light, dry and salty environments.

Be careful with cockroach bombs. A friend of mine was going overseas for a couple of weeks and let off a cockroach bomb. She forgot about Snowy the goldfish! When her friend came to feed him, he was floating on the surface, his water polluted by the chemicals from the cockroach bomb. They are toxic, so use them with care.

I once had a house with a serious cockroach problem, so I removed all the doors on the kitchen cupboards to let in as much light as possible. Bugs prefer dark to light, so this helped keep them at bay and allowed me to keep an eye on them.

HINT

If you're moving house, spray cockroach spray over all the cardboard boxes before you pack, and leave them to dry. You won't transfer your cockroach problem to your next house.

MICE

Dried snake poo placed in the corners of rooms (out of reach of little fingers) can be used to keep mice at bay. Get some from a zoo or try your local pet shop. Access points can be blocked with a wad of steel wool. You could also use a mousetrap, but rather than cheese, use a fresh pumpkin seed as bait. Mice love pumpkin seeds.

ANTS

There are two types of ant that come into homes. One type is attracted to proteins and fats. To deal with them, mix powdered borax with finely grated Parmesan and scatter it on one point along the ant trail. The ants carry the borax back to the nest and die. The other type of ant is attracted to sugars. Deter them by mixing $1/4$ teaspoon of cornflour, $1/4$ teaspoon of icing sugar and $1/2$ teaspoon of borax. The cornflour makes the icing sugar stick to the ants and they take the borax back to the nest. Scatter it on one point along the ant trail as well. Be very careful using borax if you have children and animals. If you can only see part of the ant trail and need to find the rest of it so you can locate the nest, put some talcum powder on the trail and the ants will carry it and mark the rest of the trail. If you can't use borax, find the ant nest and pour boiling water into it.

FLIES

Wipe lavender oil on door frames and window frames. You could also put 1 teaspoon of lavender oil on a small piece of sponge, add 2 tablespoons of hot water and leave this in a saucer. Top up the solution each week. Or try filling a spray bottle with lavender oil and spray trouble spots regularly.

MOSQUITOES

Keep lavender oil in a spray bottle of water and spray when needed.

If you think your cleaning is slow...

FLY POISON FROM *LEE'S PRICELESS RECIPES*, 1817

With $1/2$ ounce of sugar and $1/2$ ounce of finely ground black pepper, mix with a small amount of water to create a thin paste. Place it on a piece of paper where flies congregate. They eat it and die!

MOSQUITO DETERRENT

Mix 3 ounces of sweet oil and 1 ounce of carbolic acid. Thoroughly apply on hands, face and all exposed parts, avoiding the eyes. Do this once every half hour for the first 2–3 days until the skin is filled with it.

[This obviously assumes you don't wash often!]

HINT

Throw out any fruit that's beginning to rot because it attracts mould and bugs and will create more cleaning.

DAILY CHECKLIST FOR THE KITCHEN

· wash the dishes and put them away
· wipe down the hob and worktops
· sweep the floor
· take out the rubbish

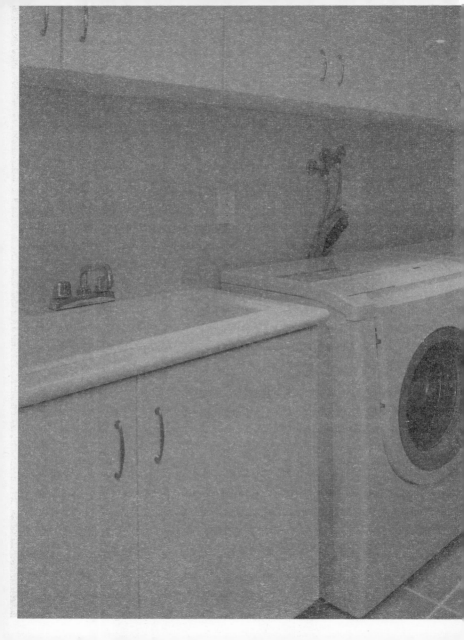

The Laundry

Your laundry may be a whole room in the house or an area tucked behind a cupboard door in the bathroom. The contents are generally the same wherever your laundry is situated – a washing machine, dryer and sink. It's important that you learn how to look after your laundry white goods and the items that go into them: all will last longer if handled with care!

How good is the washing machine? It's so much quicker than the days of using the copper, washing board and lots of elbow grease. You simply throw the dirty clothes in the machine, add a bit of washing powder, set the cycle and about half an hour later, the clothes are all clean. Imagine life without it?

The dryer is another device that has been designed to make our lives easier. Many people opt to use the dryer because they don't have a clothesline or can't be bothered hanging out the washing. But keep this in mind: sunshine is a great antibacterial!

If you think your cleaning is slow...

How to clean lace from *Lee's Priceless Recipes*, 1817

Fill a large bottle with cold water and sew around it some clean, old white muslin. Tack one end of the lace to the muslin and wrap it around the bottle taking care to have no wrinkles. With a clean sponge and pure sweet oil, saturate the lace thoroughly through the wrappings to the bottle which are to be fastened by strings in a wash kettle. Pour in a strong cold lather of white Castile soap and boil the suds until the lace is white and clean. Dry the bottle in the sun, remove the lace and wrap it around a ribbon block or press.

If you think your cleaning is slow...

TO FRESHEN CREPE *LEE'S PRICELESS RECIPES*, 1817

Wash with ox gall and water to remove dirt. Afterwards,
use water to clear the gall. And lastly, use a little gum arabic
and water to stiffen and crisp it. It's then clapped between the
hands until dried. Do not iron.

ASSEMBLE THE CLEAN KIT

Clutter bucket – to transport displaced items; **scrubbing brush** –
to scrub with; **old toothbrush** – to access tight corners;
bicarb – cleaning agent; **white vinegar** – cleaning agent;
cloth – to wipe surfaces; **rubber gloves** – to protect your hands;
broom – to sweep the floor and other surfaces.

WASHING KIT

Good-quality washing powder or liquid, Vanish, Vanish Oxi Action,
bicarb, white vinegar, dry cleaning fluid/white spirit, methylated
spirits, bar of soap, cheap bottle of shampoo and conditioner,
table salt, oil of cloves, buckets, scrubbing brush, clothes' basket.

SPEEDCLEAN

Clear anything that doesn't belong in the laundry by placing it in
the clutter bucket. Wipe the outside of the washing machine and
dryer with a cloth that's been wrung out in water. If the washing
machine and dryer are very dirty, add white vinegar to the cloth.

Clean the inside of the washing machine with bicarb and vinegar using the two-sponge technique (see page 111). It's important to do this each week to stop washing powder building up inside the machine. If there are smells, check the pipes. Pipes are really easy and inexpensive to replace. Repairing them will add to the life of your washing machine and stop solid matter getting from the pipes into the bearings. During the speedclean, check the lint catcher in the washing machine and dryer.

DID YOU KNOW? The washing machine has a lint catcher. Your washing will be cleaner if the lint catcher is cleared regularly. In front loaders it is located near the door or at the back of the machine. In a top loader, it's located either on top of the agitator or in a little bag on the side of the drum in the machine. Consult the instructions if you're not sure where yours is. Some modern machines have an automatic clearer so it doesn't need to be cleaned. If your lint catcher is on top of the agitator, put on rubber gloves and unscrew the top. It may be difficult to undo if you haven't cleaned it for a while.

If this is the case, smear the joint with a little sweet almond oil. Clear any gunk and return the lint catcher to its spot. If you have a bag, clean it out and flush with water until it's clear, then return.

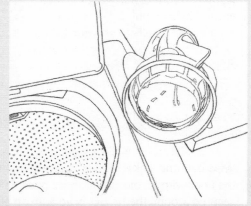

Always check the bottom of the washing machine drum in case
buttons have come loose or coins have fallen from pockets.
Create a spot in the laundry for all these bits and pieces. I have a
plastic basket that I leave on the window sill. Use whatever works
for you.

Most people know that the dryer has a lint catcher and must
be cleared before each use. Some dryers also have a water
condenser which should also be checked and emptied each time
before drying. I clean the inside of the dryer with an old pair of
pantyhose in case anything, such as plastics, have wiped against
the drum.

Be careful using the dryer with clothes that have large metal
attachments. Either remove the metal or turn the item inside
out so that the metal doesn't come into contact with the drum
and damage it.

If you use your dryer often, the area
around it, including the wall, will
accumulate lint. The best way to
clear it is with a vacuum cleaner,
using the brush attachment.

Always have
a rubbish bin
in the laundry
to collect lint.

Wipe any benches or other surfaces in the laundry by sprinkling
over a little bicarb, then spraying white vinegar on top and wiping
with a cloth.

Wipe over the sink with a little bicarb and white vinegar and mop
the floor with an old T-shirt that's been dampened in vinegar and
secured around the broom head with an elastic band.

Never store washing powder or washing liquid on the laundry window sill because they're affected by light and will make a mess. Instead, keep your cleaning items on an enclosed shelf. If they're stored under the sink, protect them from damp by storing them in a plastic container.

DID YOU KNOW? Many cloth shoes can be cleaned in the washing machine. Secure them in an old pillowcase before washing. The pillowcase protects the washing machine. Dry in the sunshine not the dryer.

STRATEGIES TO MAKE WASHING SPEEDIER

How you manage your washing will depend on how many people are in your household and how much space you have.

Have a minimum of three washing baskets: four is adequate; five is optimum. Differentiate each basket either by its shape or colour. Tying a different-coloured ribbon to each basket will do the trick. This way children (and men!) will have no trouble knowing which basket holds what kind of laundry. Have one basket for whites; another for colourfast clothes; another for dark items; another for sheets, towels and light-coloured tea towels and another for hand washing. I also have a separate basket for reds! When a basket is full, it's time to wash no matter which day or night of the week it is.

If you don't have space for all these baskets, place your washing in colour-coded plastic crates and stack them vertically.

DAILY: Stains should be treated as quickly as possible and before the clothes are sorted into the appropriate basket.

DEALING WITH STAINS

To remove grease from clothes, rub washing-up liquid into the
stain, then wash. Soak in baby oil if it's grease from the car.
To remove shoe polish, wipe the area with methylated spirits, which
dissolves the polish.
To remove fake tan, treat it as a tannin and an oil stain. Wipe with
glycerine first, then use washing-up liquid and sponge out.
To remove sun block, use washing-up liquid and water.
To remove liquid found in Fluorescent Glo-sticks, soak the item in
225 g of table salt to a bucket of cold water for about 20 minutes.
Then freeze the item. Once it's frozen, wash normally.

I like to use the warm setting on my washing machine. Use hot, but
not scalding, water for very soiled items, but be aware that hot water
puts more pressure on the fibres of your clothes. If in doubt, consult the
washing labels on your clothes. There should be a temperature guide.

HINT

Close zips before washing so they don't catch on other clothes
– it's also better for the hang of the clothes. Velcro strips should
be stuck together and the clothes placed inside a pillowcase
or washing bag, which is available at the supermarket, before
being washed. To make Velcro stick better, wet both the fluffy
and spiky sides and comb with a nit comb.

DAILY: It's fine to allow your washing to pile up but not to pile over. A
friend of mine allocates different days of the week to washing. Whites
are washed on Monday and sheets on Friday. She puts the washing
machine on as she's heading to work and puts the clothes in the
dryer when she comes home. It's part of her routine. In hot weather I
like to wash during the evening and either hang the clothes on the

line that night or early the next morning. It's okay to leave damp washing in the machine for up to 12 hours before it gets that musty smell.

If your clothes do smell musty, add 25 g of bicarb to the washing water and 60 ml of vinegar to the rinse water.

 Before putting washing in the machine, check all pockets. There's nothing worse than a tissue going through the wash and leaving white fluff on everything. If a rogue tissue spreads throughout your washing, take the

 DID YOU KNOW?
Adding a little lemon juice to the rinse water whitens clothes.

HINT

If you do all your washing in one day, make sure the first loads contain the heaviest items, such as towels, jeans or jumpers. The reason – they take longer to dry!

washing outside, shake it thoroughly and wash it again. Just make sure all the tissue is removed from the washing machine and lint filter before your next load of washing goes in. It's much speedier (and easier) to check pockets first.

PESKY PIGEONS: Coral's call to Shannon on radio

 Q: INCIDENT: 'I've got the worst problem,' reports Coral. 'Pigeons have decided to roost in the ceiling above my laundry and have pooped all over the concrete floor. I've cleaned away as much as I can but there's still white staining. What can I do?'

SOLUTION: Sprinkle some bicarb over the floor as though you're dusting icing sugar on a cake. Then sprinkle some vinegar over the top. While it's fizzing, scrub with a nylon broom. Then rinse with water. And if you want to deter pigeons, or indeed any kind of bird, buy a rubber snake around 20 cm long and place it where they can see it. They'll stay away! You could also cover the holes in the roof with chicken wire.

HINT
To remove perspiration stains, make a paste of **Vanish** powder and water. You could also mix 1 tablespoon of cream of tartar, 3 aspirin tablets and warm water. Paint on the stain, leave for 20 minutes, then wash with warm water.

HINT
Speed your mending by keeping several needles threaded with different-coloured thread in a pincushion. They're ready to be used whenever disaster strikes!

HOW SHOULD YOU CLEAN DELICATES?

A: Protect delicates by placing them in a mesh wash bag. This stops them from being flung around the machine and getting damaged. It also prevents underwire bras from getting caught in the washing machine, which can be expensive to fix.

HOW LONG SHOULD YOU SOAK CLOTHES?

A: You'd think that the longer you soak your clothes, the more dirt is removed, but this is not actually the case. Some items need soaking overnight. Others, such as delicates, should be soaked for only half an hour. Never soak woollens for more than 20 minutes because the fibres shrink when the water cools.

HINT

For clothes that have been soaked and rinsed, speed their drying by putting them in the washing machine and using just the spin cycle. This will remove a lot of the water.

SHOULD YOU WASH SOILED ITEMS WITH REGULAR CLOTHES?

A: Ideally, no, in fact, if items are really soiled, you may need to wash them a second time.

SHOULD YOU TURN CLOTHES INSIDE OUT?

A: Anything that has artwork on it, a transfer or design should be turned inside out before washing. Imagine the transfer on your favourite T-shirt hitting the metal drum of the washing machine as it washes. It can't be good for it. Anything that has a nap, such as velveteen, should be turned inside out to wash. Socks should be turned the right way out, that is, the way you wear them. They tend to be dirtier on the outside than the inside. Protect the colour of jeans by turning them inside out. Any clothes made from corduroy or velvet should also be turned inside out.

LIQUID VERSUS POWDER?

A: I prefer liquid because it's less abrasive and has less soap build-up. If you can't get liquid, dissolve the powder in water before adding it to your wash. Check the instructions for front loaders as some stipulate using powder only. I use bicarb and vinegar as a fabric softener for towels and sheets. I never use commercial ones because they irritate my skin. Wear rubber gloves when working with enzyme products because they can damage your skin.

DID YOU KNOW? To remove grass stains, use white spirit/dry cleaning fluid. A natural alternative is 1 part egg white and 1 part glycerine, which forms a soapy paste. Both have to be the same temperature when mixed, so leave the eggs out of the fridge. Leave the paste on the stain for one day then wash in blood-heat water. You could also use this recipe if you run out of soap! It's how cricket whites used to be cleaned.

HINT

Wash woollens in shampoo and rinse them in hair conditioner to keep them soft. Use 1 cap per bucket of water and always use blood-heat water.

HOW DO YOU PREVENT COLOUR FROM RUNNING?

A: Many clothes from India and Asia aren't colourfast. Check the label first. If you're not sure, test an inconspicuous part of the garment. To test for colourfastness, wring a cloth out in vinegar, place it over the garment and iron it. Colour will transfer to the cloth if it's not colourfast. Always be extra careful with red clothes.

To stop colours running, either hand wash or machine wash them in blood-heat water with table salt and washing powder. Use 225 g of salt and 1 tablespoon of washing powder per nappy bucket of blood-heat water.

LEAKY INK: Tony's call to Shannon on radio

Q: INCIDENT: 'I'm an accountant and my shirts have ink stains all over them,' says Tony. 'It's a particular problem in the top pockets. Is there a solution?'

SOLUTION: One of the best ways to remove ink stains is with rotten milk. Place some full cream milk in the sun until it forms solids. Then apply the solids to the stain until the ink starts to drift up through the milk solids. Then wash normally.

WHAT TO DO IF YOU SPILL BLEACH ON YOUR CLOTHES?

A: Match the colour with fabric paint. If you can't get the exact colour, mix the paints until you get a match. With a sable paintbrush, paint over the bleached area and feather it into the unbleached area. When it's dry, iron the back of the garment to make it colourfast.

HOW TO UNSHRINK A SHRUNKEN JUMPER?

A: For dark-coloured jumpers, fill a nappy bucket with blood-heat water and add 2 tablespoons of Fuller's earth. For light-coloured jumpers, add 4 tablespoons of Fuller's earth. Put the jumper in and gently agitate it with your hands until it's thoroughly wet. Let it sit for 10–15 minutes and then rinse completely in blood-heat water. Don't leave it for longer than this or it will bleach. Don't wring out the jumper but gently squeeze out as much water as possible. Then place the jumper on a towel in a shady spot and dry it flat. Gently stretch it back into shape as it's drying. To make the stretch more even, use two wide-toothed combs on either side of the jumper and stretch with the combs as it's drying. It's not as effective but you could also use 2 tablespoons of Epsom salts, instead of Fuller's earth, to a bucket of blood-heat water.

TO DRY LEATHER SHOES
Dust inside each shoe with bicarb and pack with newspaper or paper towel. The newspaper or paper towel will absorb the moisture out of the leather so it retains more of its suppleness. It will allow the shoes to dry back into shape without going stiff. Then polish with shoe polish.

TO CLEAN TRAINERS
Clean leather trainers with Vaseline. Clean cloth trainers by placing them in a pillowcase and washing in the machine. If you have a mixture of the two, clean the cloth part with vinegar on a toothbrush and wipe Vaseline over the leather sections.

IF YOU SUFFER FROM ATHLETE'S FOOT
Wipe tea tree oil on the affected area and rub it inside your shoes.

HANGING OUT THE WASHING

I have my washing basket at waist height on a table and keep the pegs beside the basket. Never leave pegs on the washing line because they deteriorate. If you hang your clothes as flat as possible, you'll have less ironing to do later because there will be fewer creases to deal with. Hang each item by the strongest section of the garment. Trousers and skirts should be hung from the waistband. Shirts should be hung from the tails and pegged on the side seams. Woollens are best dried lying flat on a white towel (to avoid colour transference). Towels should be hung over the line in half so that the edges sit against each other. They'll take longer to dry, but will be fluffier.

DID YOU KNOW? Bird poo can bleach your clothes because it's high in lime. Keep birds away with fluttering ribbons or CDs hung from the clothesline. Birds hate sharp movements.

IRONING

Keep your ironing board near where you use it. There are a couple of ways to speed up ironing. One way is to place a sheet of aluminium foil underneath the ironing board cover. This bounces the heat back up so you're getting twice as much heat. The other way is to iron the clothes slightly damp. The fibres are slightly relaxed and it creates more steam. If you like starch, use rice-water starch (see page 86).

WHAT CAN YOU DO IF YOU'VE GOT A MOUNTAIN OF IRONING?

Iron flat things first, such as tablecloths and tea towels, because they're easy or iron the things you hate most, then reward yourself. As soon as you have a bundle of items, put them away: it's a good visual reward. Iron shirts last because they have to be hung up. Watch TV, listen to your favourite music or do what a woman I know did; set up an ironing board across a treadmill and walk while you iron!

IF YOU ACCIDENTALLY DROP A HOT IRON ON THE CARPET

If the scorch mark is light and the carpet is colourfast, cut a cloth to the size of the burn, dip it in 3 per cent hydrogen peroxide solution and lay it over the mark for 2 minutes. Rinse with a damp cloth. If the burn is very bad, clip the surface of the wool with scissors or patch it.

To patch the carpet, cut around the damaged part of the carpet into a manageable shape with a Stanley knife. Find a piece of the carpet (perhaps some leftover or cut from somewhere little seen, such as from inside the cupboard) a little larger than the stained area. Make sure the pattern is in the same direction. Then make a paper template of the stained area and transfer this to the piece of patch carpet. Cut the patch around the template with a sharp knife. You'll need some carpet tape, which is available from carpet manufacturers, dealers and some hardware shops. Attach the tape under the edges of the damaged carpet so that the adhesive side is facing upward. Make sure that half of the tape is under the old carpet and the other half is exposed in the hole. Then press the patch carpet into the hole, sticking it to the exposed half of the tape. Brush the carpet in both directions until the fibres line up on the edges. Stand on the area for five minutes to make sure it sticks well. Then place a book on top of the patch for 24 hours.

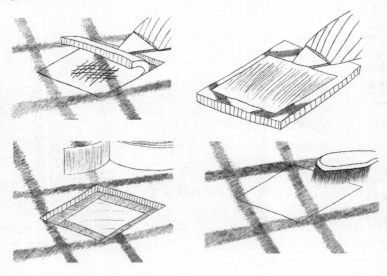

DAILY CHECKLIST FOR LAUNDRY

- sort laundry
- wash any full baskets
- iron any essentials
- empty bin

Outside

Your outside area could be a large courtyard or a modest balcony. It could be a lush garden sanctuary or a concrete square. For many people, this part of the house is an extension of their living room and an entertainment zone. It's also a sporting field, a construction site, a playground for children, a chill-out zone. Even though there are many different uses for this space, there are common themes when it comes to speedcleaning. Most obviously, it's an area that is vulnerable to changes in the weather.

If you think your cleaning is slow...

CREATE AN EVERLASTING FENCE POST FROM *LEE'S PRICELESS RECIPES*, 1817

Wood can be made to last longer than iron in the ground. Take boiled linseed oil and stir in pulverised charcoal to the consistency of paint. Put a coat of this over the timber. There's not a man who will live to see it rot.

ASSEMBLE THE CLEAN KIT

Clutter bucket – to transport displaced items; **straw broom** – to sweep; **nylon broom** – to sweep; **long-handled soft nylon broom** – to remove spider webs; **dustpan and brush** – to clean up accumulated dirt; **bicarb** – cleaning agent; **cider vinegar** – cleaning agent; **detergent** – cleaning agent; **black tea bags** – to protect outdoor furniture and freshen air; **lemon oil and peel** – to deter spiders; **oil of cloves** – to deter mould; **table salt** – cleaning agent; **methylated spirits** – cleaning agent;

sweet almond oil – to lubricate; **talcum powder** – to protect rubber; **disposable rubber gloves** – to protect hands.

SPEEDCLEAN

Clear everything that doesn't belong here with a clutter bucket. Remove spider webs by running a long-handled broom over them. Collect as much web as you can over the broom. Then put on disposable rubber gloves and use the rubber to grip the webs free from the broom. Throw the web-coated gloves in the bin. Rinse the broom in water and set in the sun to dry.

DID YOU KNOW? If you leave spider webs for too long, moisture in the webs can affect paintwork and make it flake. Deter spiders by rubbing lemon peel over the area. Speed your cleaning by putting a little lemon oil on the broom bristles before you wipe the spider webs away – you'll do both jobs in one clean sweep!

Sweep pathways with a good straw or garden broom. I use straw brooms because they're stiffer and more abrasive. Place old leaves and dirt in a dustpan and put straight into your garden waste recycling bin. I have a dustpan with a long handle and an attached broom to save on bending. If you have wooden decking, sweep with the broom. Never use detergent on unsealed wood because it will dry it out and splinter. Instead, use water and 120 ml of cider vinegar. If the area is very dirty, sprinkle a little bicarb on first, splash cider vinegar over the top, then scrub with a nylon broom while it's fizzing.

FIENDISH FOXES: Paul's call to Shannon on radio

 INCIDENT: 'We love spending time on the outside deck,' reports Paul. 'But so do some foxes. What's the best way to deal with fox poo?'

SOLUTION: Fox poo is high in protein because they are carnivorous and eat plenty of meat. Remove the protein part of the stain first with soap froth and cold water. You must use cold water or you'll set the protein. Apply the soap froth with a stiff broom then rinse with water. If the area is exposed to sunlight, shade it with an umbrella while you're cleaning because heat will set fox poo.

HINT
To stop wood going a silvery colour, put 4–5 tea bags in a bucket of hot water and mop over the area. Both wood and tea contain tannins that are attracted to each other and create colour. Tannins also help protect wood against the sun.

HINT
Move pot plants around regularly so mildew rings don't form. To remove mould on pots, apply bicarb, then vinegar and rub with a nylon brush. Rinse with water, adding a couple of drops of oil of cloves to the rinse water to inhibit mould. Leave in the sunshine to dry.

DID YOU KNOW? If snails are eating the newspaper on your doormat, wipe around the area with Vaseline. The snails won't cross it. Renew every couple of months. If there are spiders, wipe with lemon peel.

OUTDOOR FURNITURE

You need to clean outdoor furniture only when it's dirty or to tidy up before friends visit. There's nothing worse than a guest standing up to find dirt all over their new white linen trousers! Items made of shade cloth should be washed with mild soapy water. Chairs not in use should be stored under cover on an angle.

Extend the life of your outdoor furniture by storing anything that isn't weatherproofed under cover. Keep cushions in a shed, in the house, under the house or, if there's no space, in a plastic roller box that can be kept under the table. If cushions do get wet in the rain, wash them because they'll collect mildew. Add a couple of drops of oil of cloves to the rinse water to inhibit mould.

DID YOU KNOW? Whether you seal outside wooden surfaces is up to you. There are many products available in many different styles including matt and gloss. As a rule, the darker the colour of the sealant and the heavier the gloss, the more sun protection is provided.

STRATEGIES TO MAKE CLEANING SPEEDIER

As outlined earlier in Making an Entrance, one of the best ways to cut back on cleaning is to have mats at the front and back of the house. It's so easy to transport dirt from your shoes into the house, so a good mat is essential.

HINT

There are several ways to clean mouldy pathways. Check first by scrubbing the area with water and a nylon broom just in case it's accumulated dirt! If it is mould, and there's a garden nearby, sprinkle bicarb then vinegar and scrub with a nylon broom. If there's no garden, add 1 kg of table salt per bucket of warm water and scrub with a nylon broom. Pool cleaning product, **Surex Oxysure**, also works, but don't use it if there's run-off to lichen or ferns.

DID YOU KNOW? If you want to create an aged look on paths or statues, mould will grow if you add natural yoghurt to the rinse water.

UMBRELLAS

Umbrellas are best left up so they don't hoard bugs. If they are down, keep them wrapped in a cover. To clean canvas umbrellas, put 450 g of table salt or swimming pool salt in a small bucket of water and apply to the canvas with a brush or stiff broom. Allow it to dry then brush the salt crust off with a dry broom.

Never leave any rubber outside or it will perish, and always
wipe with talcum powder after cleaning.

TO CLEAN MILDEW ON CANVAS

Add 1 kg of table salt per bucket of water. Sweep it on with a broom,
leave it to dry and then sweep it off with a stiff broom. Rinse with
water if necessary, adding a couple of drops of oil of cloves to inhibit
mould growth.

FLYSCREENS

Flyscreens are a big dirt trap, so it's a good idea to clean them
well. Clean removable ones with the vacuum duster brush
attachment. Vacuum inside and outside the screen and wipe with
lemon oil or lemon peel to discourage spiders. To clean fixed
screens on windows, close the windows, damp the screen with
water then sweep with a soft broom. Rinse with a hose.

SLIDING DOORS

The runners under sliding doors are vulnerable to dirt and rust.
Clear them regularly by vacuuming any dirt between the tracks,
but not if it's wet. Never vacuum anything that's wet because it's
dangerous and could ruin the vacuum cleaner. If you want to get
rid of that squeaky noise, use a graphite puffer and lightly squirt
it along the runner.

CLOTHESLINES

The rotary clothesline is a great invention and sits proudly in
many back gardens. But be aware that if you have galvanised
wires they can rust. The best way to treat them is with rust

converter that seals the metal and forms a hard shiny surface. This
needs to be done only once every three years. Put a couple of
drops on a cloth and wipe over the wire. If you've used too much, it
will appear white. To fix it, just wipe over with methylated spirits. Rust
converter also seems to inhibit spiders, which like to live in the
anchor points
of clotheslines. The
centre mechanism
should be wiped
with sweet almond
oil every six months.
Apply it around the
gap in the crown and
put the clothesline
up and down so the
oil spreads. The great
thing about sweet
almond oil is it won't
mark your clothes,
unlike other lubricants.

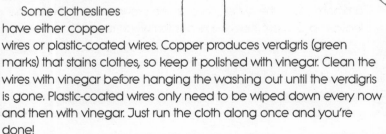

Some clotheslines
have either copper
wires or plastic-coated wires. Copper produces verdigris (green
marks) that stains clothes, so keep it polished with vinegar. Clean the
wires with vinegar before hanging the washing out until the verdigris
is gone. Plastic-coated wires only need to be wiped down every now
and then with vinegar. Just run the cloth along once and you're
done!

They're rare, but you may even have a prop line. These have two
timber supports at either end, a pivoting head and cotton sash cord
strung between. The cord has to be replaced every year because it
gathers mould.

HINT

If you've created your own clothesline using plastic cord woven backwards and forwards along a structure, stop it sagging by securing with a strap in the cord to take up the slack.

It's best not to leave pegs on the clothesline as UV rays from the sun break down the plastic and wood. Sun and rain exposure will also rust the metal mechanism. Leave them in a netted bag or basket away from the elements.

GUTTERS, DRAINS, EAVES AND AWNINGS

Get into the habit of checking your gutters three times a year. When leaves collect in gutters, they hold moisture in one spot causing corrosion and rust. And anyone who's had to replace gutters knows it's not a cheap exercise! With gloves and a bucket, climb a ladder and scoop the leaves out handful by handful into the bucket until all the leaves are cleared. You can avoid this tedious job by fitting a dome mesh guard in your gutters, which are easy to install. The guard causes most leaves to fall over and onto the ground – those leaves that do become lodged can be cleared easily by running a broom along the gutter. Once on the ground, simply sweep the leaves up and put them in the garden waste recycling bin.

HINT

Always have mesh over drains and check they're in working order – and be careful what you put down them. If you have a grease trap, make sure it is cleaned by professionals.

DID YOU KNOW? Clear a blocked drain by putting 50 g of bicarb down the pipe, then pour in 240 ml vinegar and leave for a few minutes. Flush with hot water: just boil the kettle and pour it down.

ACID WASH: Barbara's call to Shannon on radio

: INCIDENT: 'I've got some rust marks on my garage floor,' says Barbara. 'I think it's from battery acid. What can I do?'

SOLUTION: Clean the surface by sprinkling some bicarb over the area, then sprinkle vinegar and scrub with a stiff broom. Then use a descaler according to the manufacturer's instructions.

Keep an eye on your exterior paintwork. If there's any peeling paint, sweep over it regularly because moisture can get in and make the peeling spot even bigger. It's much better to have a chip than a peeling edge. Add this to your master list.

Clean under eaves and awnings and around light fittings with a nylon broom. Spiders love light fittings, but their webs are conductive and can short your lights! Add a little lemon oil to the brush of your broom and wipe over the lights to deter spiders.

DID YOU KNOW? Spiders love taking up residence in the gap between the rim and base of pot plants. Wipe the rim with lemon peel to deter them. Always wear rubber gloves when moving pot plants.

To grow moss or lichen in the garden, place 500 g of moss or lichen in a blender, add 500 ml of lager and whizz until it's a chunky lumpy soup. Splash it over areas where you want moss or lichen to grow!

Home owners should have a pest inspection every 12 months. Two of the main concerns are dry rot, which is caused by fungi and causes the drying and crumbling of wood, and woodworm, an insect larvae that also causes timber to crumble. Look out for holes at the bottom of timber. If you're concerned, contact a professional. Vigilance could save your house!

BARBECUE

It's best to clean the barbecue after using it while it's still warm. Pour a little olive oil over the hotplate and wipe with newspaper. Sprinkle over some bicarb, splash on some vinegar and scrub with a paper towel. To prevent rusting, give the hotplate a light oiling once it's cooled. If the stains are really stubborn, allow the hotplate to become super hot, apply bicarb and vinegar, then apply white sugar and vinegar. Keep the heat on until the vinegar completely evaporates, then oil the barbecue with olive oil. Turn the barbecue off, and once it's cooled, wipe it down with an old towel. The reason sugar helps is that it bonds with the dirt and burns. The oil goes under the sugar and lifts it off.

HINT

How to remove fat from pavers

What to do will depend on how bad the fat spill is. Begin by sprinkling some bicarb over the area, then splash some vinegar on top and rub with a nylon brush. Cola also removes fat, but it attracts ants. Chlorine also works, but it's very toxic. Add 1/4 tablet to a bucket of water and scrub over the spot with a nylon brush. Make sure you cover your face with a mask because the fumes are very strong. If the fat has penetrated very deeply, use plaster of Paris. Mix according to the manufacturer's instructions and apply it only to the area affected by the fat. Allow it to set, then remove. The fat will pull out with the plaster.

BINS

Organise a spot for your bins. Have them lined up according to the order they go out in, rotating them as needed. The most important thing is to make sure the handle is accessible because they can become difficult to manoeuvre when full of rubbish! Wipe lavender oil around the edge of the bin each week to deter dogs, flies and mosquitoes. Keep fleas and mites away with oil of pennyroyal, but **never use if anyone, including the dog or cat, is pregnant**. Lemon peel or lemon oil will deter spiders.

PETS

Pets' sleeping areas should be cleaned each week.
Birds – most birdcages have a tray of sand or sandpaper. When cleaning, slide the contents of the tray into a plastic bag and put it in the bin straightaway. It's okay to put the contents directly into a compost bin, but make sure you bury it or the seed will germinate. Remove the seed and water containers and put the whole cage in a wahing up bowl. Run water over the cage, gently giving your budgie a bath at the same time! If you don't have a tub, take it into the shower. Leave the cage to drain and air dry inside or outside.
Cats and Dogs – shake all the bedding thoroughly, then wash in the washing machine. If the bedding is too big, wash it in a washing up bowl with washing powder. If there are fleas, add some mint tea to the washing water. To make mint tea, add 2 teaspoons of dried mint or 3 teaspoons of fresh mint to 240 ml of hot water. Allow the tea to steep for at least 2 minutes then strain it. Also spray the bedding with mint tea or oil of pennyroyal. **Do not use oil of pennyroyal if anyone in the house, including the pet, is pregnant**. After washing these items, always clean the filters and lint catchers in the washing machine.
Fish – clean fish tanks with an old stocking. Just wrap it over your hand to make a mitt and wipe along the inside of the tank. You

could also buy some suckerfish, which are known as 'vacuum-cleaner fish', to make cleaning speedier. If you've got an outbreak of algae, check the filter. It may need flushing or replacing. Also check that it is big enough for the tank. Be careful when adding water to a fish tank because sudden changes in temperature can kill the fish. If the water level has dropped and you have to add some more, fill a plastic bag with fresh water, let it sit in the remaining tank water until it becomes the same temperature, then add it slowly to the tank.

DID YOU KNOW? You can stop gates and hinges squeaking with sewing machine oil. Add a couple of drops to the noisy hinge.

If you get tar on your clothing, remove it with baby oil. Just rub the baby oil into the tar until it melts, then add detergent and wash.

FENCES

Clean according to the type of fence it is: most only need to be swept over if they're grotty. Be careful with cutout timber, which can rot if exposed to the weather. Wash with detergent and water applied with a broom.

WINDOWS

Cleaning windows is a spring/autumn-cleaning job and I think it's best left to a professional. To clean them yourself, add 240 ml of methylated spirits to half a bucket of water then transfer to a spray bottle. Spray the solution onto the glass and wipe with a squeegee. Polish with paper towels if needed. Don't use newspaper to clean windows. Newspaper was a great cleaner when the ink was made of lamp black but these days the ink has a latex base and will leave smear marks on the glass. One of the frustrating things when cleaning a window is working out which side of the window a smudge is on. To deal with this, use vertical stripes on the outside of the window and horizontal stripes on the inside of the window. You can tell which side of the window the smudge is on by the direction of the stripes. The reason to use vertical stripes on the outside of the window is because that's the direction rain falls so when it rains, it won't leave streaks against the window.

LAWNS

A garden always looks tidier if the grass is mown. Long, stray grass going everywhere screams unloved and unkempt. If you're short of time, tidy the area by raking up any big leaves. Then work a stiff garden broom over the grass to tidy it up. It's like giving the lawn a hair-do. I know it sounds strange, but it works.

If you have the option, choose trees and plants that don't drop their leaves. Alternatively, don't place your outdoor furniture under trees and plants that do drop their leaves.

HINT

A good hedge along the edge of your garden helps to settle road dust and acts as a filter.

RECYCLING

Many people have lost the art of recycling. So much stuff just gets thrown into the bin. It's very easy to get into the habit of reusing materials and one of the best ways is to create a space for recycled items. I keep an area near my back door for items that can be recycled and reused. The garage is another good spot. Just make sure the area is under cover and protected from the weather.

One of the easiest things to recycle is glass jars. Just clean them when you do the daily washing up and store them in your recycling area. Remember: if you're going to use them to store food, you need to sterilise them. Heating the jars in a hot oven is the best way to do this.

Reuse old tins: you could store old cooking fat in them, they are handy containers for nuts and bolts and you could even use them to soak paint brushes in.

Egg cartons are great for germinating seeds. They're even better for holding children's paints. See if your local primary school or craft centre would like your old ones. You could also take them back to the farm shop where you buy your eggs and reuse the carton – many are pleased to do this. Plastic squeeze-top bottles make great paint containers for kids. Keep bits of old string, tie them together and roll them into a ball. That way you'll have string ready to use whenever you need it. Keep elastic bands in a container to use again. Cereal cartons can be recycled into filing trays. Decorate them to become storage for children's toys.

Keep plastic bags and store them in a plastic bag holder. This is a fabric tube with elastic at either end and a loop to hang it from. You stuff new bags in the top and pull out old bags from the bottom. Plastic bags can be washed over and over.

Plastic takeaway food containers can be used for so many things. They're particularly great for keeping leftovers in, then doubling as a lunch box. Wash them and reuse them.

You could even recycle old leather shoes to become pot plant holders!

GARAGE/SHED

When organising a garage or shed, put tools you use most often near the door. There's nothing worse than rummaging around in a space and creating more mess. Have bins for rags and dust cloths and always have a rag bag. The best way to store tools is with a shadow board — it means you can identify your tools at a glance. You can even create your own shadow

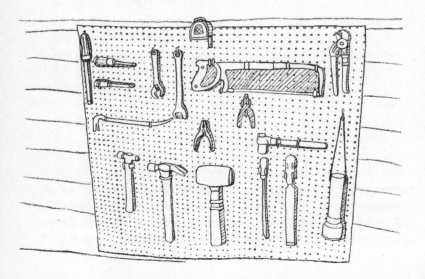

board by installing hooks along the
wall, making an outline of the tool
and painting the spot. Other items,
such as nails and screws, should be
stored in labelled jars. If you have
lots of shelving along the walls, fill
them with containers. You can use
takeaway containers or old ice-
cream containers. Have labels you
can see at a glance and read from
every direction. Make sure your
shelves are very sturdy. Reinforce
free-standing shelves by placing
them back-to-back and bolting
them together.

Large power tools should be kept together in a dry area. Don't
wrap the cords around the power tools or you'll create kinks. The best
way to store electric cords is to hold one end in the space between
your thumb and forefinger and wind the cord over your elbow, then
back up to your thumb and down again to your elbow until it's
coiled. Wind the remaining cord around the top of the coil and plug
the two ends together to protect the pins and stop insects taking up
residence in the holes. Store the cord inside the cardboard centre
from a roll of paper towel.

If the shed is damp, elevate the area by placing an old wooden
pallet or bricks on the ground, then add new flooring on top of the
pallet or bricks. Keep fuels, chemicals and flammable materials on
metal or masonry shelving. Never store them on ground level
because they're more likely to come into contact with water that will
corrode the cans and cause dangerous spills. Don't place them
above eye level either because it is much easier to have accidents
when reaching up high. They should also be kept out of direct

sunlight. Make sure these materials are in non-corrodible un-breakable containers, are marked clearly, have childproof caps and are out of reach of children.

HOW TO SPEEDCLEAN A CAR

I don't enjoy cleaning the outside of a car and generally go to a car wash, but I do have suggestions on how to speedclean the inside. One of the best ways to cut back on cleaning is to ban people from eating or drinking in the car. If your children are able to hold their own food, they're old enough to wait until the end of the journey before eating. They can drink water. I have bottles stored in the backs of the seats, along with a small packet of tissues and zip-lock bags, in case of emergencies. If you do spill anything, deal with it as soon as possible. Keep some paper towel and wet wipes in the glove box. Clean any plastics in the car with glycerine applied with a cloth. If someone vomits in the car, the best thing to do is to remove the seat from the car, clean it, apply bicarb, dry it in the sun, then vacuum and return it to the car.

HINT

If there's a smell in the car

Remove the smelly item, then dampen a tea bag in water and add a drop of lavender oil. Find the vents that feed the air conditioning – they are generally located under the dashboard – and leave the tea bag there for a while. If you can't find the vents, leave the tea bag anywhere in the car. The tea works because it kills dust mites and mildew, and the lavender particles are small enough to get into the air conditioning and leave a fresh smell. Some car manufacturers add fragrance to their air conditioning: now you can do it yourself!

Spring and
Autumn Cleaning

The spring and autumn cleans are the perfect opportunities to reorganise your house. It's a bit like a department store stocktake: twice a year reassess and renew each room in the house. Spring and autumn cleaning is about tackling all the tasks you missed or avoided doing during the year – so look where you don't normally look, high and low. It's a chance to rearrange furniture to suit the seasons, freshen carpets or use some new bedding. It's also a good time to unearth items you don't need or use any more, and to get rid of them so that they are not left lingering in the house and gathering dust. Charities often organise home collections and are happy to take items, including toys, books, knick-knacks and clothes you no longer want.

Begin with the master list that you've been adding to during the weekly speedcleans. Organise and tackle your chores room by room.

ENTRANCE, HALL OR LANDING

If you have a hallstand, clear all items and vacuum inside the drawers. If you want to freshen up the space, consider a new plant or decoration.

When spring cleaning the linen cupboard, I use a trolley to store the items I've removed from the linen cupboard. Find out what needs mending and set it aside. Vacuum the shelves inside the linen cupboard. Replace lining on your shelves. Then shake and refold each item before returning it to the cupboard.

The linen cupboard should be sorted by having items most used at eye level, those least used on higher levels and items for children, such as towels, on lower levels.

Clean light shades and stands. Clean brass and metal arms with a good-quality brass polish.

Clean paintings. **Acrylic** paintings can be cleaned with a damp cloth. **Water colours** should be cleaned by a professional. To remove residue and dust from **oil paintings**, clean with stale urine, salt and potato. This technique is a guaranteed conversation stopper! Collect 1 litre of female urine and leave it in the sun for a week to reduce to 500 ml. Add 1 tablespoon of salt and 2 tablespoons of grated raw potato. Stir and allow the mixture to sit for 30 minutes. Dampen a cloth in the mixture, wring it out and then wipe gently over the painting. Dampen a clean cloth in water and wipe the painting gently and pat it dry. You can also rub brown bread over the painting to clean it but it can induce mould if the atmosphere is damp, so don't use this technique if you're in a damp, dark spot. For any serious cleaning problems, see a restorer. Never use alcohol-based cleaners such as methylated spirits or turpentine on **gilded frames**. Most gilding is covered with a layer of shellac and alcohol-based cleaners will affect it. Instead, dust the frame with a hairdryer on the cool setting. This should be enough to clean it but if dirt remains, wipe a damp cloth over the frame and then dry it with a soft cloth.

LOUNGE, DINING, FAMILY ROOMS AND STUDY

A key focus during the spring and autumn cleans is to rearrange furniture to maximise breezeways. In the warmer months, you want air to flow. In the cooler months, you want air to be retained.

Give sofas and cushions a good whack, remove cushions and vacuum all the crevices. Change cushion covers or wash existing covers. Clean the underside of tables and chairs where spider webs lurk. Do the same with chairs. Shampoo carpets and rugs. Clean blinds and curtains. Remove covers from light fittings and clean them. Give lampshades a really good clean. Sort out your bookshelves. Take all the books out, clean the shelves, dust each book and recycle the ones you don't want any more. Either take them to a second-hand shop or donate them to a school fete. Return borrowed books. Dispose of any old magazines or recycle them for the kids to make cutouts with. Dispose of any videos or DVDs that don't work any more. Sort out your CDs. In the study, deal with bills and paperwork. Catch up on filing.

BEDROOM

Remove all the clothes from the wardrobe and vacuum inside. Go through your clothes and decide which ones will stay, which ones go into the rag bag and which ones can be donated to charity. If there are some quality garments, try selling them online. Audit your clothes without being wasteful. Keep this in mind – if you have clothes you don't wear, it's either because they're out of fashion or you don't like them. If you don't like them, don't keep them. Determine which clothes need mending. Then organise summer clothes at one end of the wardrobe and winter clothes at the other end. If you have enough room, store the off-season gear elsewhere. Sort through your shoes, too. If they're damaged, have them repaired or throw them out. Hang a new muslin bag filled with lavender in the wardrobe to ward off nasties. Wash the duvet and change all the blankets on the bed. If you like, change the duvet cover to give the room a completely new feel. Wash blankets every six months or when they become dirty. Make sure you get under the bed and clean it well. Clean the curtains, blinds and windows. Shampoo carpets and rugs.

BATHROOM

There's actually very little to spring clean in the bathroom. The main task is to clean out the cabinets. Remember the rule – a place for everything and everything in its place. Go through your medicine cabinet and throw out items that are past their use-by date.

KITCHEN

This is a big job. Begin by cleaning the cupboards. Do it cupboard by cupboard rather than all at once or you'll create a huge overwhelming mess. Remove items and clean the shelves. Vacuum inside drawers. Throw out or recycle anything that's chipped or broken. If you have problems with bugs, either spray cupboards with insecticide or use non-toxic alternatives. If you use insecticide spray, wait 1 hour before putting items back. Go through the pantry and check use-by dates. The same applies to food in the freezer. Also check your cleaning products and get rid of anything you don't use. Clean the filter in the oven hood. Clean blinds, curtains and windows.

LAUNDRY

Clean out your sewing kit. Remove the tail end of threads and little bits of fabric.

OUTSIDE

Clean out the garage or shed. Return borrowed items and retrieve anything you've lent. Clean outdoor furniture. Clear gutters, drains, eaves and awnings. Clean the clothesline. Organise pest inspections. Clean windows either yourself or hire a professional. To clean them yourself, add 240 ml of methylated spirits to half a bucket of water then transfer to a spray bottle. Spray the solution onto the glass and wipe with a squeegee. Polish with paper towel if needed. Don't use newspaper to clean windows. Newspaper was a great cleaner when the ink was made of lamp black but these days the ink has a latex base and will leave smear marks on the glass. One of the frustrating things when cleaning a window is working out which side of the window a smudge is on. To deal with this, use vertical stripes on the outside of the window and horizontal stripes on the inside of the window. You can tell which side of the window the smudge is on by the direction of the stripes. The reason to use vertical stripes on the outside of the window is because that's the direction rain falls so when it rains, it won't leave streaks against the window.

WHEN YOU'VE FINISHED

When you've finished the spring or autumn clean, reward yourself and the family – because cleaning should be a total household effort. Go out for dinner or throw a dinner party to show off your gleaming newly cleaned house.

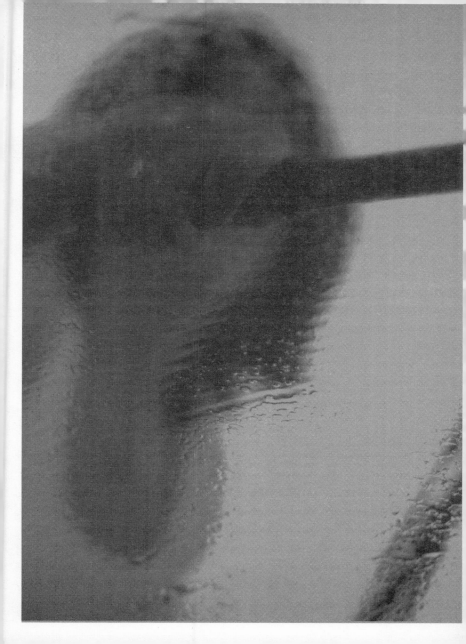

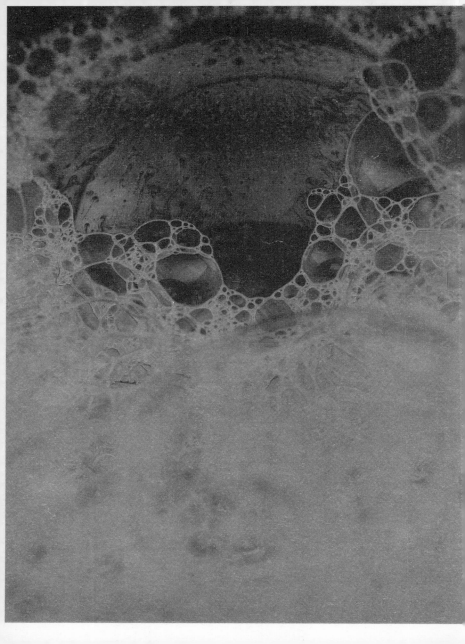

Organisational Do's and Don'ts

When dealing with a stain, a lot of people think that they can improvise. After a spill, they head to the cleaning cupboard, pick what they believe might work, and give it a go. When that doesn't remove the stain, they try something else, then when that isn't successful, they bring out another product and on it goes until they end up making an even worse mess. Keep in mind that every time you add another chemical, you change the stain's chemical signature. For example, if you spill red wine on the carpet, clean it with bicarb and vinegar as described in this book; however, if you've mistakenly used soda water, then a spot remover, you can't then just use bicarb and vinegar because the stain signature has altered. You're no longer dealing with a simple red wine spill – you have to remove the new stains you've created in addition to the red wine stain! The take-home message from this is: first, work out what the stain is, then what the surface is and fix it.

WHOOPS! AND WHAT TO DO NEXT…

Here's a checklist of things to consider before tackling a stain.

Work out what the stain is made of: is it protein, fat, chemical/biological dye or resin/glue?

Know what the surface is – the kind of fabric, flooring, worktop etc. that you've stained.

Know the appropriate chemicals to use to remove the stain. If in doubt, speak to an expert. Try to minimise the number of chemicals you use.

Unless you know it will work, always do a test patch first. It's a good practice run!

Never spot clean stains on your carpet within four weeks of it being steam cleaned. Vacuum the carpet four times before you spot clean it as spot cleaning stains can adversely react with steam cleaning chemicals.

Never use excessive water or moisture on carpet. More is not better!

Wear appropriate clothing, such as gloves, goggles and mask, especially when using heavy chemicals.

Don't make chemical mixes you don't understand. Mixing certain chemicals can create toxic fumes. You could add one chemical to another and create a toxic fume, ruin a surface or even have an explosion!

Remove stains as soon as you notice them. Don't wait – they become harder to shift with time.

Stain-removal solutions are not interchangeable. You can't use advice relating to carpet on your woollen jumper. Every surface is different.

There is no substitution or approximation. If you don't know, get expert help.

HOW TO REMOVE BASIC STAINS

Protein stains are one of the trickiest to remove because you must not use heat, detergents or many commercial spot removal products on or near them. If you do, it sets the stain. It's just like cooking an egg, which goes hard as soon as you add heat. Many proprietary cleaning products will set protein stains. The best way to remove protein stains is with facial soap, cold water and, if it's on carpet, a little water. Scrub soap on the stain, then blot it with paper towel until it has been removed. Protein includes any animal product such as blood, gravy, meat, eggs, cheese and milk, and seeds and beans. Once you remove the protein part of the stain, you can then apply heat to remove other stains.

Oil, grease and fats include vegetable oil and butter. The best degreaser is washing-up liquid. You can see how it works when detergent is added to a greasy sink! Be aware that fat stains are often combined with protein stains. If food has been cooked in oil, or has fat in it, such as a lamb chop, the protein part of the stain has to be removed first. Make-up generally contains lots of oil too; detergent is the solvent to use. The best way to determine oil stains is by rubbing the stain between your fingers – fat and oil make your skin slippery and shiny. To remove them, use detergent and warm water. Only use the tiniest amount of water on carpet or upholstery.

Carbohydrates are starches and sugars. They're found in potato, rice and paper glues. The best way to deal with these stains is to allow them to dry, then brush or vacuum them out. For example, if you spill rice on the carpet, remove any solids, pat the area with paper towel, leave to dry then vacuum. If the stain has any other component, such as salt, dilute with a little water first, then apply the process described above. For sugar stains, add a little vinegar or a little detergent to help break them down.

Inks, paints and dyes require a solvent. Vegetable dyes, such as those found in artificial or naturally coloured foods, are best removed with sunshine. If you can't get the stain in the sun, use an ultraviolet light which can be hired from the chemist. Sponge the area with a small amount of equal parts lemon juice and water then aim the ultraviolet light over the stain. Check the stain every 2 hours until it fades. Some vegetable dyes oxidise, which means they respond to oxygen in the air – like a cut apple turning brown on its surface. As they oxidise, a tannin stain is produced. Remove tannin stains by wiping with a little glycerine, leave for 15 minutes then sponge out with a cloth that's been wrung out in vinegar. Repeat until the stain is gone. The glycerine takes the stain backwards in time a little. This procedure is particularly good for beetroot stains. Again, if the stain is on carpet, don't use too much moisture.

To remove **paint stains**, you need to know if the paint is water-based, acrylic or oil-based. For children's water-based paints, remove with soap and water. For acrylic house paint or tube paint, use methylated spirits. If oil-based, use white spirit/dry cleaning fluid.

Resin stains require a chemical solvent. For apoxy resins, use acetone. You must use acetone and not nail-polish remover. Take care using heavy chemical solvents. Be mindful that the solvent may break down surfaces around the stain. For example, white spirit/dry cleaning fluid will break down paint, so only apply the solvent to the stain itself, rather than the surrounding area. Be careful how much you use.

PREVENTION IS BETTER THAN CURE

It's a well-known phrase, but a good one. Ask yourself before you embark on an activity: what can go wrong and how can I prevent it? Try to anticipate potential stains and put into place measures to avoid them. For example, for high dirt areas, spray carpet with Scotchgard (this works on shirts as well); use old newspapers on the tops of cupboards to capture grease and grime. Don't do things like serve spaghetti bolognese on white shag-pile carpet – you're just asking for trouble! Create specific areas for doing messy jobs. For example, clean shoes outside or on several layers of newspaper.

And remember: when removing stains from carpet, always rinse chemicals out after you've cleaned. This applies even with basic chemicals such as vinegar and milk. If you don't, you'll be left with bad smells and more stains.

When doing the laundry, prevent disasters by reading the labels on your clothes. Use the recommended washing temperature. If the information isn't included on your clothes, I recommend washing in warm water – unless there's a protein stain. If there's a protein stain, wash in cold water. Warm water relaxes the fibres and makes cleaning easier. To avoid shrinkage, use the same water temperature in the wash and rinse water. Wash woollens in blood-heat water.

For new garments, put the iron on a cool setting in case the garment contains a fibre, such as elastin, that reacts with heat. You don't want to end up with a shrivelled shirt! Never iron clothes with any stains on them because you will set the stain.

THE BIGGEST DO OF ALL

Since cleaning is essential for a healthy comfortable lifestyle, make it fun: stick a smile on your face and do it together.

QUICK GUIDE TO REMOVING STAINS

Below is a kind of ready reference or quick guide to stain removal from fabrics:

Beer (including lager)	Paint a paste of Vanish Oxi Action on the stain and leave for 15 minutes. Then wash normally.
Beetroot	Treat with glycerine before washing normally.
Bird droppings	Wash fabric normally.
Blood	Wash fresh bloodstains through the washing machine on the cold setting. If you can't, use cornflour and water. For old bloodstains, use cold water and soap.
Chewing gum	Harden the gum with ice and cut as much off as possible with scissors or a blade. Then apply dry-cleaning fluid with a cotton wool ball, sprinkle talcum powder to absorb it and work the remaining gum out by rubbing in circles.
Chocolate	First clean with soap and cold water. Then clean with soap and hot water.
Coffee or tea	For fresh stains, use glycerine applied with cotton wool, then wash in washing powder. For old stains, use glycerine, then dry-cleaning fluid and detergent.
Deodorant	Use dry-cleaning fluid before washing.

Egg yolk   Use soap and cold water first, then washing powder and warm water.

Fruit juice   Use detergent and sunshine. For stone fruits and fruits with a high tannin, treat the stain with glycerine first.

Grass   Use dry-cleaning fluid before washing in washing powder.

Grease and oil   Detergent suds. For heavy staining, soak in baby oil first.

Hair dye   Dry-cleaning fluid or kerosene, or hairspray if you can get to the stain immediately.

Ink or ballpoint pen   Rotten milk or dry-cleaning fluid. Use glycerine first on red ink.

Lipstick and make-up   Dry-cleaning fluid

Milk   Wash normally on cold cycle.

Mud   For red clay mud, apply dry-cleaning fluid then wash. For black mud, wash in the washing machine.

Nail polish   Apply acetone, not nail polish remover.

Paint   For water-based paint, use methylated spirits. For oil-based paints, use turpentine.

Rust   Use a descaler or lemon juice and salt.

Sap   Apply dry-cleaning fluid.

Shoe polish   Use methylated spirits.

Soft drinks   Treat as though it's a fruit stain because soft drinks are made of vegetable dyes.

Sweat   Make a paste of Vanish Oxi Action and water and leave on the stain for 15 minutes before washing normally.

Tar   Use baby oil, kerosene or dry-cleaning fluid.

Urine   Wash in washing powder and dry in sunshine.

Vomit   Washing powder, sunshine or Napisan, washing machine and dryer.

Wax   Ice, dry-cleaning fluid, talcum powder.

Wine   New red wine – vinegar.
Old red wine – glycerine, bicarb and vinegar.
White wine – vinegar.

INDEX

Cleaning Lists

MASTER LIST

Chore	Last Completed	Next Due

SHANNONS MASTER LIST

Chore	Last Completed	Next Due
Chimney sweep		
Carpet cleaning		
Video head clean		
Windows washed		
Ink toner and paper refilled		
Squeaky locks and hinges		
Insect extermination		
Minor repairs		
Wash doonas and pillows		
Equipment service		
Turn mattresses		
Spot stains		
Scratches		
Mending		
Polish silver		
Shoe repairs		
Replace moth bags		
Replace tools and kit items		
Clean drains		
Inspections		
Lawns cut		

WEEKLY SPEEDCLEAN

Day	Rooms	Kit	Who
Monday	Bedroom		
Tuesday	Lounge / Dining		
Wednesday	Bathroom		
Thursday	Kitchen		
Friday	Family / Study		
Saturday	Outside		
	Entrance		
	Laundry		
Sunday	Nothing		

SHANNON'S WEEKLY SPEEDCLEAN

Day	Rooms	Kit	Who
Monday	Bedroom	Clutter bucket, clothes basket, spray bottle, vacuum cleaner, damp cloth, dry cloth, furniture polish cloth, detergent, beeswax, lemon peel, methylated spirits, lavender oil, elastic bands, broom, paper towel, old T-shirt and rags.	
Tuesday	Lounge / Dining	Clutter bucket, bicarb, vinegar, methylated spirits, furniture polish, lavender oil, lemon oil, cloth , dusters, paper towel, insecticide spray, spray bottle, hair dryer, small soft paintbrush, broom, vacuum cleaner	
Wednesday	Bathroom	Clutter bucket, bicarb, vinegar, *Gumption*, water, methylated spirits, cloth (such as an old T-shirt), old stockings, nylon broom, dustpan and brush, vacuum cleaner, mop, bucket, rubber gloves, spray bottle, old toothbrush, nylon scrubbing brush, *CLR* or *Ranex*, denture cleaner, lavender oil, oil of cloves, glycerine, detergent, old towel, paper towel, rags	
Thursday	Kitchen	Clutter bucket, bicarb, vinegar, detergent, glycerine, vanilla essence, table salt, spray bottle, vacuum cleaner, damp cloth, methylated spirits, lavender oil, old T-shirt, elastic bands, broom, sponge, old stockings, old tooth-brush, paper towel, rags, garbage bags, storage box, dishwashing brush	
Friday	Family / Study	Clutter bucket, bicarb, vinegar, methylated spirits, furniture polish, lavender oil, lemon oil, cloth , dusters, paper towel, insecticide spray, spray bottle, hair dryer, small soft paintbrush, broom, vacuum cleaner	
Saturday	Outside	Clutter bucket, straw broom, nylon broom, long-handled soft nylon broom, dustpan and brush, bicarb, vinegar, detergent, tea, lemon oil and peel, oil of cloves, table salt, methylated spirits, sweet almond oil, talcum powder, disposable rubber gloves	
	Entrance	Clutter bucket, bicarb, vinegar, water, methylated spirits, cloth (such as an old T-shirt), straw broom, dustpan and brush, vacuum cleaner, mop, bucket, rubber gloves, Scotchgard, hairdryer, spray bottle, insecticide	
	Laundry	**Clean Kit:** Clutter bucket, scrubbing brush, old tooth-brush, bicarb, white vinegar, cloth, rubber gloves, broom **Washing Kit:** Good-quality washing powder or liquid, *Napisan*, *Napisan Oxygen*, *Napisan Plus*, bicarb, white vinegar, dry cleaning fluid/white spirits, methylated spirits, cake of soap, cheap bottle of shampoo and conditioner, table salt, oil of cloves, buckets, scrubbing brush	
Sunday	Nothing		

DAILY CLEAN

Room	Chore	Who
Bedroom	Make the bed	
	Put away clothes and remove dirty clothes	
	Empty bin	
Lounge, dining, family rooms and study	Put away any projects	
	Sort mail	
	Collect any crumbs	
	Empty bin	
Bathroom	Wipe the sink and bath with rolled up pantihose	
	Use the toilet brush	
	Check there is toilet paper	
	Empty bin	
Kitchen	Wash the dishes and put them away	
	Wipe down the stove top and bench tops	
	Sweep the floor	
	Take out the garbage	
Laundry	Sort laundry	
	Wash any full baskets	
	Iron any essentials	
	Empty bin	

MAGNETS

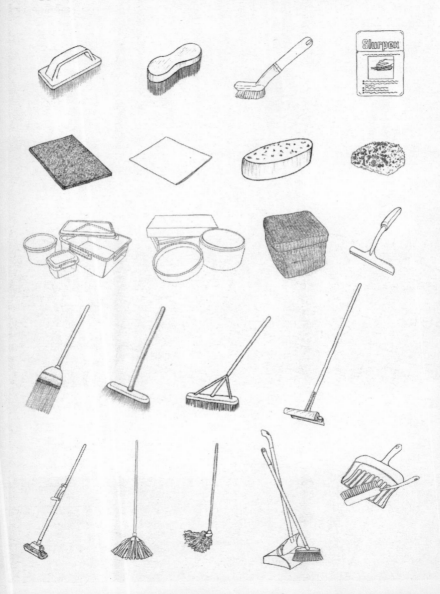

Moveable Furniture Plans

FURNITURE (scale 5mm = 25cm)

LOUNGE, DINING AND FAMILY ROOMS AND STUDY

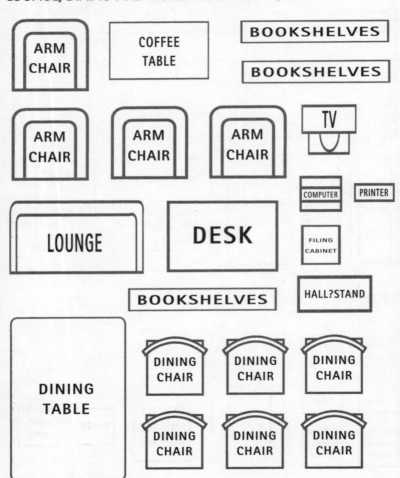

THE BEDROOM

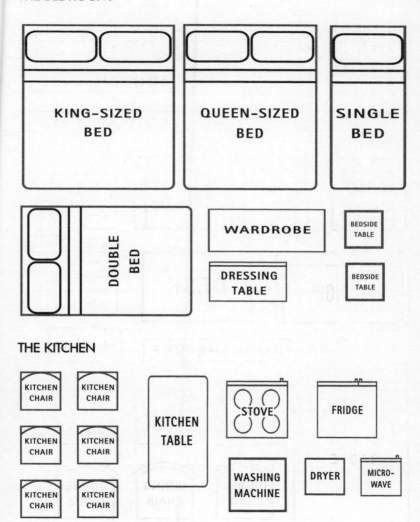

KING–SIZED BED

QUEEN–SIZED BED

SINGLE BED

DOUBLE BED

WARDROBE

BEDSIDE TABLE

DRESSING TABLE

BEDSIDE TABLE

THE KITCHEN

KITCHEN CHAIR

KITCHEN CHAIR

KITCHEN CHAIR

KITCHEN CHAIR

KITCHEN CHAIR

KITCHEN CHAIR

KITCHEN TABLE

STOVE

FRIDGE

WASHING MACHINE

DRYER

MICRO-WAVE

Scale: 4 squares = 1 metre

Scale: 4 squares = 1 metre

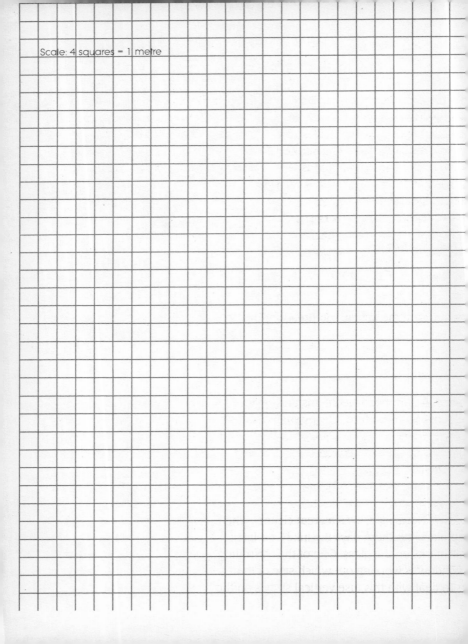

Scale: 4 squares = 1 metre